MINISTRY IDEABANK No. 2

JOHN H. KRAHN
AND
BETTY JANE FOSTER

C.S.S. Publishing Company, Inc.
Lima, Ohio

MINISTRY IDEABANK II

Krahn, John, 1943-
  Ministry ideabank number two.
  1. Church work — Miscellanea. 2. Theology, Practical — Miscellanea. I. Foster, Betty Jane, 1924- . II. Title.
  BV4400.K73 1986   253   85-30866
  ISBN 0-89536-801-3

Copyright © 1986 by
The C.S.S. Publishing Company, Inc.
Lima, Ohio

All rights reserved. No part of this publication may be reproduced, stored in a retrieval system, or transmitted in any form or by any means, electronic, mechanical, photocopying, recording, or otherwise, without the prior permission of the publisher. Inquiries should be addressed to: The C.S.S. Publishing Company, Inc., 628 South Main Street, Lima, Ohio 45804.

6819 / ISBN 0-89536-801-3   PRINTED IN U.S.A.

Table of Contents

PREFACE 5

ADMINISTRATION 7
   General 9
   Office Aids 15

BAPTISM 21

CARING MINISTRIES 25

CHRISTIAN EDUCATION 31
   Sunday School 33
   Vacation Bible School 39
   Adult Education 40

CHURCH YEAR 43
   Advent 45
   Christmas 47
   Lent 53
   Easter 58
   Pentecost 60
   All Souls / All Saints / Reformation 61
   Special Services 62

COMMUNITY INVOLVEMENT 63

CONFIRMATION 67
   General 69
   Instruction 71
   Parental Involvement 75
   Rite of Confirmation 76

EVANGELISM 77

FELLOWSHIP 81

FUND RAISING 87

MISSION AND MINISTRY 93

NEW MINISTERS (MEMBERS) 97

PASTOR / PARISHIONERS RELATIONSHIPS 141

PUBLIC RELATIONS 107
    Internal 109
    External 112

SENIOR CITIZENS 113

STEWARDSHIP 117

WEDDINGS / MARRIAGE 123

WORSHIP LIFE 127
    General 129
    Creative Worship 134
    For the Children 136
    Liturgy 138
    Music / Choirs 139
    Prayer 142
    Sermons 143
    Summer Worship 144

YOUTH 147

MISCELLANEOUS 153

Preface

Thanking God for the success and positive reader response of the first *Ministry Ideabank* book, we have compiled a second anthology of great ideas to enhance parish ministry. From throughout the United States and parts of Canada, from overseas in Norway, from down under in Australia, clergy, professional church workers, and laypeople have continued to share their new and exciting ministries. With great joy and humble hearts we can now pass them along to you in *Ministry Ideabank II* — hundreds of great, *new* ideas to enhance every aspect of parish ministry. It is our earnest prayer that our readers will again find many fresh and creative ways in which to serve God's people in their churches and in their communities.

All preparation for this manuscript was accomplished on a volunteer basis. A special thanks to Ms. Gay Borley of Trinity Lutheran Church, Hicksville, New York, for assisting us in the initial compilation. We are also deeply grateful to everyone whose contributions of ideas has made this second edition possible. Royalties received from all sales of this book will be donated to the church-at-large in gratitude to God and to his glory.

                                            Betty Jane Foster
                                            John H. Krahn

ADMINISTRATION

ADMINISTRATION
General

Plan for Parish Planning

A new idea was used for a Parish Planning Meeting this past year. Council members suggested that the pastor put together as many ideas as possible *(hopes and dreams, old and new methods)* for ministry in the areas of stewardship, etc. I came up with six pages of ideas which were developed briefly into goals *(and methods to reach those goals)*. The council invited leaders and auxiliary groups to attend the parish planning meeting and asked them to rank the ideas for priority. This gave excellent feedback to take to specific boards for planning and carrying out their ministry in the year ahead. *(Rev. Francis M. Lieb)*

Joint Council Workshops

A cluster of Lutheran churches within one geographic area gathered their church council members for a workshop and a chance to share concerns and procedures. We discussed responsibilities of council members, dynamics within a council meeting, and leadership styles. As a result, there was a growth in unity between the churches. The leaders found that other councils shared similar troubles and rewards. They also had a chance to think about the way they were doing their jobs. *(Rev. Gary Hedding)*

Wish List

After our church budget has been determined, we often come up with needs like materials, equipment, furnishings, and emergency projects not included in the budget. We either have to make the difficult decision to wait until next year's budget is drawn up or we add the item to our wish list.

We consistently post and publish the wish list and have found that people are willing and able to meet many of these needs with gifts over and above their regular giving. Some people consider

ADMINISTRATION
General

these items as suggestions for memorial or thanksgiving offerings. In addition, we have received contributions for wish list items from persons outside the congregation. *(Rev. Dr. Rodney L. Broker)*

Easy Energy-Saver

Your church may be able to save energy as well as money by simply shutting off unneeded lights burning in gas appliances. I was astounded to count no less than thirteen (13!) pilot lights burning up gas in heaters, furnaces, and the kitchen range in our facilities, and doing it 24 hours a day, 365 days a year.

While most of the pilots were needed during the heating season, we found that we could cut off four in our kitchen range with no more problem than posting a sign to that effect. When the heating season was over, we turned off all but one pilot — in the water heater.

Your situation may not be as bad as ours, but you might discover that your church can exercise better stewardship of both resources and funds by some judicious "turning off." *(Rev. Richard W. Schick)*

Beat the Budget

Whenever we find the church needs ANYTHING, before we commit budget funds (planned or unplanned), I make a note of it in our bulletin and/or newsletter. Before we'd only list items that were typically used as memorial gifts, but now we're including everything from a typewriter to a dehumidifier to the cost of a week's lawn mowing. People give enthusiastically when they know that there are tangible results. And they do not reduce their pledge. *(Rev. James R. Pierce)*

ADMINISTRATION
General

Don't Forget to Remember

I've got a memory like an elephant — grey and fuzzy. I will think of a meeting I have to schedule, a phone call I need to make, or an item to put on my "things to do today" list, but by the time I get to my office I've forgotten half of what I planned to do. Now I carry a relatively inexpensive mini-cassette recorder and tape each idea as it occurs to me. When I return to the office, I transcribe them onto my "to-do" list. I'm in good shape if I just don't forget to take the recorder with me. *(Rev. Daniel H. Mangler)*

Sunday Dinner for Voters

Our congregation has a Voters' Assembly every two months. Because of the long distances some of our members travel, we decided years ago that Sunday would be the best time for Voters' Assemblies. We join for a potluck dinner in the fellowship hall immediately after worship. After the dinner, we hold our meeting. This practice has resulted in a great deal of fellowship among our members, and our attendance at Voters' Assemblies is equal to churches five times our size. *(Rev. Richard Finck)*

A Personal Ministry . . . Nothing is Routine

I think every aspect of our ministry should be stamped with our own unique personality *(cleaned up a bit by Jesus Christ)*. So often we hear pastors complaining of the tedious tasks — writing bulletins, etc. Why not make each bulletin a masterpiece of telling the Gospel, as well as giving valuable information? I never write an acceptance transfer letter without thanking the congregation for the person received; telling how they are doing, wishing blessings upon the ministry of the brother, reminding him of Jesus' love. Can't some trivial tasks be transformed into meaningful expressions? I don't have the time *not* to do it. Why not be orthodox in doctrine and very unorthodox in style *(instead of the other way*

ADMINISTRATION
General

around)? We all have different gifts. One of yours is yourself. *(Rev. John Kenreich)*

Do You Know Where . . .?

Often the question arises whether or not I know how to get to a particular hospital. This is especially true when one of our more active members is hospitalized. In order to provide this information as quickly and accurately as possible, I have a number of 3" x 5" cards with the name of the hospital and the directions whether traveling from the north, south, east, or west. Not only has this made things easier for others but also for myself, especially when I travel to certain hospitals infrequently. I plan to expand this index to include other points of interest such as funeral homes, social service organizations, and churches in our area. *(Rev. Frederick M. Raap)*

Write It Down

Have you ever heard a good joke or anecdote or perhaps read a particularly interesting insight and said to yourself, "I'll have to remember that," only to forget it later. When I come across something I want to remember, I write it down on a 3" x 5" card and then file it in a box on my desk. Every few months, I go through it to reacquaint myself with what I've collected. This has been helpful to me for my sermons, in teaching, and for writing newsletters. *(Rev. William E. Shimkus)*

Can't Get One Try Two

When our church membership grew, we needed a full-time secretary. It was difficult finding a person with the required skills who would work for the salary our church could pay. The problem was solved by hiring *two* part-time secretaries. One of them works

ADMINISTRATION
General

Mondays through Wednesdays, and the other Thursdays and Fridays. Both are highly competent, and both only want to work part-time. We divided up the work so that each knows her own responsibility. Everyone is pleased with the result. *(Rev. Cecil Murphy)*

Official Reports Bulletin Board

Parish members have a right to see the monthly treasurer and financial secretary's reports as well as to read the minutes of the governing body of the congregation. Rather than print these in full in our newsletter, our congregation has a "For the Record" bulletin board. Copies of these reports and minutes are posted as well as copies of the planning sheets which list the year's goals set by the parish boards. *(Rev. Henry A. Simon)*

Furnishing a Church

If you are building a new facility and furnishing it as well, get a breakdown of all the individual costs and suggest that members each select a certain item to purchase. We did this with all items inside our church when it was remodeled, and it was completely furnished in no time. *(Rev. Michael Lutz)*

Spaced-out Elections

When holding elections at parish meetings, begin the voting early in the meeting and continue until the election process is completed. Do this as the regular business is being conducted. A lot of time is wasted if all voting and ballot counting is done as a separate agenda item. *(Rev. John K. Kjoller)*

Note Taping

A good seminar is more valuable if you can bring home a set of very complete notes for later reference. My cassette recorder

ADMINISTRATION
General

has a start/stop button on the microphone cord. I whisper my notes softly but clearly with the microphone about an inch from my lips. The volume level is set at the normal recording level. I edit and transcribe my whispered notes as soon as possible. Your secretary can aid you in the transcription process. *(Rev. Philip J. Bohlken)*

Let All Keep Silence

We've lined our pew racks with small pieces of foam rubber to enable our hymnals and Bibles to be replaced into the racks quietly. The foam absorbs the noise and protects the books. *(Rev. Charles Naugle)*

Charting the Church

Churches can be hard to find at times, especially for people who have recently moved into the area. I have found that printing a map with the church location on the back of my business card has been most helpful. *(Rev. Gary L. Danielsen)*

(See PASTOR/PARISHIONER RELATIONSHIPS "Sharing Joys and Sorrows")
(See PASTOR/PARISHIONER RELATIONSHIPS "Parishioners Visit Pastor")

ADMINISTRATION
Office Aids

If You Can't Afford It . . . Share

At a meeting of the local ministerial association one of the pastors mentioned that the local school district was offering an electronic stencil cutter for sale. He wondered whether anyone else might be interested in jointly buying the cutter to make printing needs a bit easier. Another member said, "If we buy it then we'll only be about ten years behind everyone else instead of twenty-five." That comment became the impetus for a look at a plain paper copier. What resulted was the purchase of a plain paper copier for ten churches. The volume made us spend a little more money, but with the money came more options on the machine. We have based the machine at a congregation which is centrally located and now are up-to-date with our publications. The cost was $500 for each church and two cents per copy for maintenance. We couldn't even get the stencil cutter for that price. *(Rev. Kenneth Kaufmann)*

Cooperative Newsletter

Our parish has an electronic stencil cutter — a real blessing for saving time and waxing creative with the monthly newsletter and Sunday bulletin. One way we have saved extra time for our typist is to request that any articles submitted for our newsletter (or bulletin) be typed, if possible, but no wider than the publication can handle. We will occasionally copy a neat, legible, handwritten article or report. Those submitting articles are encouraged to include any fancy headings, drawings, cartoons, etc. which might enhance their articles. This method has not only pleased the typist but also the writers. (Their submitted material appears exactly as they intended and is never edited.) The readers do not have to read a whole newsletter in the same type face or style of writing, and the result is a more cooperative spirit. The newsletter, which is called "Together We Can," is owned by the whole parish and not just by the pastor, typist, or editor. *(Rev. John R. Anderson)*

ADMINISTRATION
Office Aids

For Pastors Without Secretaries

When I select hymns, responsive readings, and sermon topics (by the season), I type dummy bulletins on scratch paper so that in a given week, all I have to do is add announcements and type the stencil. Without a secretary, my time can get crammed full when a funeral or extra counseling crops up. This assures me the bulletin won't take too long to complete. *(Rev. James Pierce)*

Answer Phone

As the church office is in our home, we had a phone answering machine installed to give us some privacy during mealtime. Many of the calls came at Christmas and Easter when people ask about service times. Now I use a longer, outgoing message and let the answering machine give information on service times and formats. A recorded greeting for the holiday and background music appropriate to the season can also be included. People can still reach me on our home phone if they really need me. *(Rev. Philip Bohlken)*

File/Retrieve Journal Articles

Most pastors subscribe to one or more professional journals. But how do you find a key article you have read a year or two ago? Every summer, when things in the church office are slow, hand your secretary the issues you've received during the past twelve months. She can type the author, title, journal, and date of each publication on a separate index card. You can then easily file the cards by subject. When you really need that item on "The Political Import of David's Marriages" (Journal of Biblical Literature, December 1980), you will be able to find it in your file under "1-2 Samuel." *(Rev. Mark I. Wegener)*

ADMINISTRATION
Office Aids

Imprinted Postcards

Our congregation finds that 3½" x 5½" card stock with our church name and address imprinted thereon have several uses. These postcards (reverse side blank for a message) provide a less expensive alternative to a letter when sending notices about meetings, reports needed, etc. They also encourage deacons calling on inactive members and evangelism visitors to leave a written note when the persons aren't home when they call. I find the cards ideal for leaving a brief message when I visit a hospital patient who is out of the room for tests. *(Rev. Henry A. Simon)*

ADMINISTRATION
Office Aids

Building a Sketch File

To get extra mileage out of the stencil sketches used in parish papers and bulletins, each individual sketch is cut from the master when it is received from the stencil sketch service and filed in a small (3½ x 6½") envelope. The sketch imprint is pasted on the upper left-hand corner of the envelope. On the upper right-hand corner, the appropriate heading is marked, i.e., world hunger, choir, fellowship. After a sketch has been used, it is blotted clean, cut out of the stencil, and returned to the file envelope ready for re-use.

Whenever a good black and white sketch is noticed in some reading material or in the mail, it is pasted on a sheet of 8½ x 11" paper. When the page is full, we run an electronic stencil cut of the composite and then cut out the individual sketches, placing them in our sketch file envelopes for future use. *(Rev. Fred D. Dommer)*

Filing Ideas for Illustrations

Stencil illustrations can be stored easily in the popular "self-adhesive" photo albums. Locating a suitable illustration from accumulated unused stencil inserts is often a time-consuming task, but when placed in the photo albums and arranged according to categories, it is easy to look over the available supply and make a choice. The same system works for illustrations used on off-set and electronic stencil machines. *(Mrs. Ellen L. Puotinen)*

Tickler File

Make two copies of outgoing correspondence. File one in your subject file and the other in a looseleaf notebook, in chronological order. This "tickler file" is easily referred to when you want to recall how you answered a particular letter, the date the message was sent, etc. It also saves time in searching the files, especially if your secretary has misfiled the letter. *(Mrs. Betty Jane Foster)*

ADMINISTRATION
Office Aids

Used Paper Gift

An insurance company near our community gives us free paper. Every other month we pick it up from their printing department. Usually this paper is made up of scraps . . . leftover promotional pieces (with one side clear), odd shapes, some punched for use in a three-ring binder. Our volunteers sort the paper, and we use it for bulletin inserts, our calendar, and our church council. All in all we get eighty reams of "free" paper a year thereby freeing our offerings for mission work. *(Rev. James Steinbrecher)*

Scrap 'n Save

I haven't bought notepads for a decade. Since we always seem to have overruns from our mimeographing, I take some of the scrap paper, cut it in half, and staple it into notepads. I use the halves to write notes to parishioners, to my secretary, to the officers of the church. The full-sized sheets can be used for sermon notes and rough drafts of Bible studies, etc. *(Rev. Wendell Henkenmeier)*

Calendar at Hand

Taping a copy of the current month church calendar on the wall above the typing table near the phone in the study keeps it handy for ready reference while conversing on the telephone or composing at the typewriter. Each month is taped on top (page-by-page fashion) so I can look back a month or two, if need be, without pulling a file. *(Rev. W. O. Neisch)*

Witness-by-Mail

Purchase a year's supply of the religious issue postage stamp at Christmas and use them on your mail year-round for a Christian witness. *(Rev. John K. Kjoller)*

ADMINISTRATION
Office Aids

(See PUBLIC RELATIONS/External "Canvass by Mail")
(See SENIOR CITIZENS "Seniors Contribute Significantly")
(See WORSHIP LIFE/General "Bulletin Fillers")
(See WORSHIP LIFE/General "Never Caught Short")

BAPTISM

BAPTISM

Cradle Roll Shepherds

Our parish is divided into several zones shepherded by laypersons who are called deacons and deaconesses. When a child is baptized, the deacon and deaconess of the zone where the child lives are present along with the parents and sponsors. They are then charged with keeping in touch with the family and the child over the years. They remember the child at special times throughout the year (birthdays, Christmas, Easter, etc.) At the age of three, the shepherds encourage the parents to enroll the child in Sunday School and to avail themselves of other Christian educational agencies. *(Rev. A. F. Volmer)*

Baptism Anniversary Prayers

We try to keep complete records on the Baptism dates of persons associated with our congregation. Each week during the Prayer of the Church we include, by individual name, those who will mark their baptismal anniversaries during the coming week. In the prayer we thank God for the living witness of these saints and pray for the Spirit to strengthen and direct their daily ministries. The congregation is also encouraged to remember these individuals in their personal prayers on the day of the anniversary.

We have found that such a remembrance in prayer is comforting and encouraging to our people. They are reminded of the significance of their "day of adoption" and are encouraged in the practice of daily baptismal affirmation. It also adds a regular section of celebration and thanksgiving to the prayers in addition to those for persons in crisis or illness. *(Rev. Dr. Rodney)*

Symbolic Installation

At a recent installation of our Church Council officers, we tried a simple way to demonstrate the importance of their Baptism to their tasks. After thanking the retiring offiers, I read each new officer's name and asked them to group around the baptismal font. Assuring them that this was not a rebaptism and that it was only

BAPTISM

a symbolic demonstration of the important identity God had given each of them at their Baptism, I dipped my finger in the font and spoke the name of each person as I touched their foreheads with my wet finger. I then read Romans 6:3-10 in which St. Paul speaks so beautifully of the significance of Baptism. The incumbents were asked if they were willing to accept their commission. After their affirmation, we congratulated them and gave them the Benediction. *(Rev. Virgil R. Anderson)*

Picture Cradle Roll

We purchased a Polaroid camera in order to take pictures of the babies with their parents at the time of Baptism. The child's name, birthday, and baptismal date are written at the bottom of the photo along with the parents' names. This makes it more interesting for all who come to view the pictures. They can immediately identify whose child is on the cradle roll. When the child is three years old, the parents receive the picture and are invited to enroll their child in the nursery Sunday School class. *(Rev. Ivan R. Amman)*

CARING MINISTRIES

CARING MINISTRIES

Going One-On-One

Recently we have adopted a new program as part of our ministry of shepherding. It is a system of one-on-one relationships involving people who have similar life situations and a need to talk. It is particularly helpful for those individuals undergoing a major transition in lifestyle or facing a crisis. To get it started, we solicited people who were willing to share their experiences with another person currently going through the same experience. We then matched these individuals with those who needed an empathizer. Some of the circumstances that are being shared are: cancer, loss of job, death of parent/spouse/child, anorexia, divorce, and amputation. This program has helped the people in our congregation who needed a loving, compassionate person who has been there. What a tremendous ministry for all involved! Those in need receive the opportunity to talk and be comforted and reassured by someone else who knows what it feels like to be in those shoes. Those willing to share get the fulfillment of having been a friend to a hurting brother or sister. *(Deaconess Brenda L. Neitzke)*

Care Group Ministry

Besides ministering to the spiritual needs of our people, we believe that we should also be concerned with their physical needs. As a result, we have about fifty people who visit our members in the hospital; offer members rides to church, the grocery store, the post office; rake leaves; put up storm windows; and provide meals to families who have experienced a birth or death in their family or have a mother who is in the hospital. The blessings of this program have been experienced by the members of our congregation. *(Rev. Bill Majer)*

Caring Conversations

How do you let people who don't attend church know you miss them? After years of highly detailed, involved, and unsuccessful

CARING MINISTRIES

shepherding programs, we hit upon an idea that spreads care across a broad base and allows the worshiping congregation to become more caring. On the first Sunday of each month, we distribute cards to those at worship with the names and telephone numbers of all members who weren't in church the previous month. The cards have instructions on the reverse side for a simple telephone conversation. The people at worship (families) are asked to make ONE telephone call. It is a simple method for concerned Christians to show their care for one another. It doesn't involve a lot of time. It reaches a maximum number of people. What do you suppose would happen if you did this for a year? Right! People would begin to get the idea that their church really cares about them. *(Rev. Lowell L. Siebrass)*

Advising the Bereaved

Sometimes in the haste of preparing for a funeral, a family who particularly desires a headstone on the grave of their loved one, unfortunately purchases a plot in the memorial park section of a cemetery. It would be helpful to point this out to your people as part of your ministry to the bereaved. Europeans especially feel strongly about this and are not always aware of the increasingly common practice of internment in memorial parks. *(Rev. Leonard R. Klein)*

Using Ma Bell

Here is one simply way to "visit" hospitalized members on a Sunday morning. When our organist begins the prelude, I telephone a patient who can then hear the sounds and the voices of the worshipers. The line stays open for about ten minutes, and then I call another. You'd be surprised how pleased they are. By the way, this also prevents the telephone from ringing and going unanswered during worship. *(Rev. Thomas A. Daniel)*

CARING MINISTRIES

Postcards of Love

Here's an idea with a Valentine's Day emphasis but good for any time. Distribute a postcard to worshipers and encourage them to jot down thoughts or feelings of love . . . kind words and expressions that they would like to have someone share with them. Ask everyone to take their cards home and address them to someone they appreciate. It's a good way to practice the Golden Rule. *(Rev. Edward Arle)*

Youth Sermons for Older Folks

If you are running out of interesting ideas and object lessons for devotions at the Nursing Home, try sermons that are designed for children. Sometimes things need to be changed, but on the whole there is a great wealth of ideas, illustrations, and objects that can be used. The residents really enjoy and appreciate something different too. *(Rev. Wayne P. Gollenberg)*

(See ADMINISTRATION/General)
(See ADMINISTRATION/Office Aids)
(See CHURCH YEAR/Advent)
(See CHURCH YEAR/Christmas)
(See CHURCH YEAR/Lent)
(See CHRISTIAN EDUCATION/Sunday School)
(See COMMUNITY INVOLVEMENT)
(See CONFIRMATION/Instruction)
(See PASTOR/PARISHIONERS RELATIONSHIPS)
(See WORSHIP LIFE/General)
(See WORSHIP LIFE/Prayer)

CHRISTIAN EDUCATION

CHRISTIAN EDUCATION
Sunday School

Sunday School Personal Touch

In order to encourage attendance in Sunday School, one of our teachers sends a weekly letter to the class. The letter includes subtle suggestions for studying for the next week's lesson and some personal notes. The children look forward to these letters addressed just to them, and if the teacher misses one week, they call him to see what happened to their letter. Attendance has increased in the class, and even those who do not attend are provided with some Bible lesson for the week. *(Rev. Philip E. Hemke)*

Time Off for Teachers

Most Sunday Schools are set up in such a way that the teachers never have a chance to attend the adult class on Sunday mornings. This year we have two teachers for each Sunday School class. Each one teaches for three weeks and is then off for three weeks. This accomplishes three useful goals: (1) it allows teachers to attend adult class on their time off; (2) it gives the children a good model and demonstrates to them that Sunday School is also important for adults; (3) if one of the teachers is away, there is another teacher who is familiar with the lessons.

When we introduced this system, we found more people were willing to teach. *(Rev. Edward J. Grant)*

Sunday School Down Under

Our Sunday School in Nambour, Australia, is small. As a variation of one teacher — one class, we have team teaching for grades three — six with four teachers participating. There are about twenty-five children in this group. While the children sit on the carpeted floor, each teacher presents a portion of the lesson. One begins with the theme-setting activities (song, prayers, and talk); another presents the story (using sketched posters); then one teacher amplifies on the story to help it penetrate; finally, the application is taught. Activities, singing, etc., fill in the rest of the time. The teachers like it, and all the children are most enthusiastic. *(Rev. Paul R. Gerschwitz)*

CHRISTIAN EDUCATION
Sunday School

Bridging the Gap

We do not have sessions of Sunday School during the summer, but we try to keep in touch with the kids through periodic mailings. Our first contact with them is by sending each youngster an appropriate booklet which we purchase from the American Bible Society — the material is well done, attractive, and inexpensive. The second mailing is an invitation to a mid-summer Sunday School Picnic. The third is a reminder that our fall classes are about to begin and asks them to think about bringing a friend to class. The feedback from the kids has been exciting. They like to get their own mail, even if it is only from the church. *(Rev. Wendell Herkenmeier)*

Kaleidoscope

During the summer, we offer an alternative Sunday educational program called *Kaleidoscope*. Except for a class set up along more traditional lines for children aged three through grade two, the offerings are generally open to all ages. Families have the option of attending one of the offerings as a unit, or the members may pursue individual interests. Offerings include a film festival (one movie each week, followed by discussion); arts and crafts (usually four opportunities lasting three weeks each); and a study/discussion group (geared primarily to adults).

This year we are planning a six-week puppet workshop for grades three through eight. Individuals and families are free to move from one offering to the other during the summer. Members are also able to attend several Sundays, go on vacation, and still come back to the same or different activity. Refreshments are available in all class areas. Our people have responded favorably to this rather relaxed atmosphere, yet we have been able to offer Christian growth opportunities throughout the summer. *(Rev. Trenton R. Ferro)*

A Child Bearing Gifts

During our regular worship service, we have a child from the

CHRISTIAN EDUCATION
Sunday School

Sunday School walk up with the offering basket full of gifts given during the opening Sunday School devotions. The child accompanies an adult usher who brings the regular worship offerings forward. This not only gives more visibility to our Sunday School during worship services but also gives the children who participate an exciting sense of being an important part of worship. How proud many little children are to walk up to the altar with their own daddies! *(Rev. Joel J. Brauer)*

Cheerful May Baskets

Last year our Sunday School children constructed their own May baskets. On May Day, parents and teachers took the children to the homes of all our elderly and shut-in members to deliver the baskets. On each basket was a handwritten note telling them how much Jesus loves them. We had a wonderful response. One lady was so touched that she wrote a letter to the children and made a generous contribution to the Sunday School! It helped the children practice, in a simple way, what they learn in Sunday School about serving the Lord with gladness! *(Rev. Joel J. Brauer)*

Sunday School TLC

The names of our members who are hospitalized are given to a Sunday School class on a rotating basis. The children make get-well cards which the teacher sends or, if possible, takes personally to the hospital. Two things are accomplished. The class is made aware of a concern outside themselves, and the patient is touched and encouraged by this show of love and concern. *(Rev. Arno H. Meyer)*

Anticipating Sunday School

We invite all parents to bring their Pre-Sunday Schoolers to the opening sessions of Sunday School on the last two Sundays of the school year. They sit with the children of the Nursery/Kindergarten section, hear the stories, and sing the songs. In the fall, when these new students begin Sunday School, there is less cause to be fear-

CHRISTIAN EDUCATION
Sunday School

ful or tearful as they already know what to expect. *(Rev. Louis Hermansen)*

Sunday School Feud

One of our fifth grade Sunday School teachers, a fan of the TV program "Family Feud," created a feud with the class. Weeks before the big event, our teacher passed out questionnaires to all the Sunday School teachers, pastors, and members of the congregation and used their answers for the **Sunday School Feud**. The feud was held during Sunday School with all other classes and parents invited to attend. It was a big success. The children learned more, the parents were impressed by what their children had done, and everyone had a wonderful time. We awarded prizes and then voted for the mission project to which they wanted to go. *(Rev. Philip E. Hemke)*

(See FUND RAISING)
(See BAPTISM)
(See WORSHIP LIFE/For the Children)
(See WORSHIP LIFE/Creative)
(See WORSHIP LIFE/Summer Worship)
(See CHURCH YEAR/Christmas)
(See CHURCH YEAR/Easter)
(See CHURCH YEAR/All Souls, etc.)

CHRISTIAN EDUCATION
Vacation Bible School

Symbolic VBS Welcome

Here is a fail-proof way to take the trauma out of Vacation Bible School registration and a method to communicate with children at a level which helps them feel welcome.

On the first day of VBS, class rosters which include the teacher's name, the age level of the class, the classroom number, and names of the children in each class are placed in the entrance hallway. They are made of poster board using large print and the roster for each class has a symbol painted on it. Last year, one three-year-old class had a daisy and another class had a tulip. The four-year-olds used symbols of butterflies, trees, and bluebirds, five-year-old classes pictured a child, a lamb, and a heart. Attached to the bottom of each poster board roster were tags for the children printed with their names and the appropriate symbol for the class in which they were enrolled.

Each teacher wears a name tag with the class symbol, and below the room number on each class door a picture of the symbol is attached so that the children who are too young to read numbers can identify their room from the picture.

Two volunteers help parents and children find their names on the class rosters. (Extra name tags and registration forms were available in the entry hallway.) In addition to being an efficient method of class registration, the use of the rosters and symbols were a colorful introduction to Vacation Bible School which said to the children, "We're happy that you came." *(Rev. George F. Lobien)*

Day Camp Replaces VBS

We hold a one-week, all-day Day Camp for our children in grades three through seven instead of the traditional Vacation Bible School. The advantages are in the type of activities which you can do that can't be accomplished in the shorter hours of VBS and in the fellowship which is built through the longer time spent together. The adult leaders choose the materials during a twenty-four hour "overnight" the week before Day Camp. Members skilled

CHRISTIAN EDUCATION
Vacation Bible School

in special crafts come in for one-and-a-half hours on two of the days to lead the children in making projects.

One special feature is a field trip. We have traveled to a Christian radio station *(with a stop for ice cream)*, visited an old graveyard to do tombstone rubbings, toured a local Nursing Home, and spent one entire day at an Arboretum.

Periods of "quiet time" are part of the daily curriculum when the children can meditate on assigned portions of Scripture and when staff can converse with individual children about their own personal relationship with Jesus. *(Rev. Mikell Peratt)*

VBS Slide Show

As part of the closing worship for Vacation Bible School, we present an unusual slide show with all the children and teachers starring. During the first two or three days of VBS, candid shots are taken of everything and everyone, including: projects being made, books and curriculum being used. You just have to be shutter-happy and let your imagination fly. The slides are developed in forty-eight hours, and it only takes a few days to put together a show. Children *(of all ages)* like to see themselves on the screen, and it's not too difficult to tie in the theme of our VBS with the slides. *(Rev. Wayne P. Gollenberg)*

VBS for the Special Child

We offer a special class, taught by one of our own members who is trained in special education, for the educable mentally retarded children in our rural county. The class is held at the same time as our regular week-long VBS, and the children who attend get the chance to interact, play, and worship right alongside these special children. Most areas have some kind of parents association for retarded children. Publicize through that group and through the local newspaper. Many fine materials for classroom teaching are available through Lutheran publishing houses. *(Rev. Joel Brauer)*

CHRISTIAN EDUCATION
Vacation Bible School

Supervising VBS

To help us in our Vacation Bible School program, we have a superintendent and an assistant superintendent each year. The assistant is recruited with the understanding that she will be the superintendent the following year. This allows her to receive on-the-job training the first year. The next year she knows what needs to be done, and she can then train the person for the following year. *(Rev. Ken Lampe)*

A VBS Money Saver

This year our handicraft project was to make banners on newsprint. I got an end roll from the Akron Beacon Journal, and then tore off sections in six-foot lengths. We provided colored marking pens, yarn, construction paper cut into various sized pieces, and Elmer's glue. The children used their imaginations, taking themes from the week's lessons (Christmas, Easter, Ascension, etc.), and we ended up with over forty banners. All of them were hung up for display in our education building, and the result was a couple of festive weeks! *(Rev. Thomas A. Daniel)*

(See WORSHIP LIFE/Creative Worship)

CHRISTIAN EDUCATION
Adult Education

New Style/New Member Class

Scheduling an adult information/instruction class that runs between six and ten weeks so that every interested person can attend is something of a problem. Therefore, I have been holding my adult instruction classes in seminar form. We meet on a Saturday from 9 a.m. to 5 p.m. with a five-minute break every hour, and lunch is provided by the evangelism committee. I give a copy of my notes to each person in attendance to help them follow along. At the end of the seminar, those who wish to become members of the church are assigned three things. 1) They must first work through approximately 100 questions based on the material presented at the seminar; 2) they are required to read through *Luke* and *Acts*, answering about sixty questions from a worksheet as they go through the material; and 3) they are required to read a book on the Christian faith such as *The Hidden Discipline* by Martin Marty also using a worksheet with questions to help them pick out the most important material. About four to six weeks after the initial seminar, we meet as a group to go over the questions they have answered on the worksheets and to clarify difficult points of theology. The last meeting runs for three hours. After this, they are proposed for membership in the church. This is especially effective with people who have had some previous Christian background. *(Rev. John E. Kassen)*

Adult Class Shepherds

Many pastors conduct a class similar to my "Dialogues in Christianity." They are made up of adults, members, and non-members, and meet two hours each week for ten to twelve weeks. There is no emphasis on church membership, but at the end of the course, non-members are invited to join.

What is unique about our program is that the class becomes a shepherding group once our ten-week course is over. A president and shepherd are elected from within the group. The shepherd is a special "assistant" to the pastor. The president is automati-

CHRISTIAN EDUCATION
Adult Education

cally appointed to the membership board. The group selects its own name, meets once a month, and sponsors an activity each year for the entire congregation. *(Rev. Orlyn G. Huwe)*

Bible Study for Mother and Child

As the mother of a toddler who needs me on Sunday mornings as well as during the rest of the week, I had difficulties with church attendance. Our family of five has always attended worship services and Bible School on Sunday. But there is no place for the mother who must take care of her preschool child during the Sunday School hour. A toddler's noise is not appreciated in the adult Bible class, and the alternative of staying home during that time does not set a good example for the older children in the family. After speaking to our Board of Elders and the superintendent of the Sunday School, we set up a class for mothers with babies. The room contains a couple of rocking chairs, a crib, and toys. Our mothers change diapers as needed, nurse or bottle-feed, and finger foods are provided for the more active toddlers. The class is slow paced but with the idea that we can study His Word together in Christian Fellowship while also fulfilling our God-given role as mothers. *(Mrs. Barbara Rozek)*

Personal Decision

Since people attend our Adult Instruction classes under no obligation to join the congregation at the conclusion of the session, I often had difficulty helping these people make the transition from the classes to church membership. When the course ended this past spring, I gave each of them a listing of approximately twenty times when I would be available to meet with those who were interested in church membership. The idea worked very well. The burden for making the appointment was with the prospective member, and they were inviting me to talk to them about joining the church. I did not get the feeling that I was twisting anyone's arm

CHRISTIAN EDUCATION
Adult Education

or intruding into their lives. *(Rev. Marcus J. Miller)*

Sunday New Member Classes

Holding adult inquiry classes during the Sunday School hour has worked well in our congregation. The following advantages to such scheduling are: 1) Lay leaders can teach the adult Bible class while the pastor teaches the inquiry class; 2) class participants do not have to come to church at another time during the week (Some may be coming on Sunday to drop off their children for Sunday School.); 3) members can be encouraged to attend before or after their worship as a "refresher"; 4) Sunday morning "going-to-church" habit is encouraged in prospective members; 5) the final session, which introduces our congregation to prospective members, includes a visit to our other Sunday morning adult classes who invite the newcomers to become involved in the Christian education hour. *(Rev. Henry A. Simon)*

Mustard Seed Very Small Indeed

While conducting a study/discussion series on Jesus' parables, we discussed the mustard seed parable (Mark 4:30-32). I passed around a packet of mustard seeds for each person to take one. For a Sunday Worship emphasis, tape a mustard seed to each bulletin. *(Rev. Paul Walley)*

(See FELLOWSHIP)
(See WORSHIP LIFE/Creative Worship)
(See WORSHIP LIFE/Summer Worship)

CHURCH YEAR

CHURCH YEAR
Advent

"Parents Nights of Freedom"

On Friday evenings, from 7-10 p.m., in November and December (with free babysitting provided), we hold "Parents Nights of Freedom." This is provided as a service to parents in order that they may do Christmas shopping for the children or just get away for an evening of relaxation. A sign-up sheet is circulated on several Sundays prior to these evenings. Older members of the congregation whose children are grown provide the babysitting. A variety of programs are planned for the children. *(Rev. Roy A. Steward)*

Advent Journey

A few years ago, my wife heard a good idea for increasing our children's anticipation of and involvement in the celebration of Christ's birth. During Advent, our children help Mary and Joseph — figures from our creche — travel to "Bethlehem" (wherever the nativity scene is set up, on a mantle or under the tree) from "Nazareth" (a distant place in the house, perhaps a far corner of the basement). Each day the children move the figures, symbolizing their journey. On Christmas Eve they join the other figures at the Nativity scene, and the child Jesus figure appears too. The focus on the coming of God's great Gift, Jesus, is natural and central. *(Rev. Frederick W. Reklau)*

St. Nicholas Family Potluck

On the Sunday closest to the feast of St. Nicholas, December 6, we hold a family potluck at noon. It is an opportunity to sing Advent hymns and talk Advent customs. We have had plays, skits, puppet shows, and always an appearance from St. Nicholas who gives gifts to children. A little research on lives of the saints will yield background on the Bishop of Myra (c. 342) who, among other distinctions, is the patron saint of children. *(Rev. Richard C. Hintz)*

CHURCH YEAR
Advent

Paint Your Windows

The seasons of Advent and Lent can be embellished with colorful window paintings. A talented artist in the congregation or an art teacher at a local school outlines the scenes or symbols with white tempera paint. Youth of the confirmation or high school classes (or any group) can use their imagination in colorfully painting the sketched designs. Bright colors such as yellow, orange, pink, lavender, and peach show up better than red, blue, green or brown. Of course, a snack of hot chocolate and cookies helps make the project enjoyable as well as a witness of the faith. *(Rev. Dr. Peter Mealwitz)*

(See PUBLIC RELATIONS/Internal)

CHURCH YEAR
Christmas

Jubilee Christmas

Rather than playing hero with other persons' kids, the Lafayette Urban Ministry has created a program called Jubilee Christmas which will be duplicated this year in six area churches. New toys are purchased and brought by individuals and church groups to a specifc church location. Needy families, screened and approved by LUM, are invited to come and select toys for their children. Toys are provided to average three toys per child, with three children per family. Babysitting is set up, and there are wrapping tables where parents can have the toys gift-wrapped if they wish.

Before the parents select their toys, they meet together with a pastor who talks about the value of both giving and receiving. As each family will be receiving toys, they are invited to give either time to LUM or the host church, or to give a cash contribution to some world relief need.

In addition to the toys, each family receives a gift certificate for the equivalent of a sack of groceries and a canned ham or turkey. Good, used clothing is also available, and gift certificates are provided for teenage children. Refreshments (donated cookies, coffee, and punch) are served during Jubilee.

A church, assisted by several nearby congregations, can handle thirty families in a personal, helpful way. Children, youth, and adults can all be involved. The program has worked exceedingly well for three years benefiting *everyone!* *(Rev. Gary L. Reif)*

Givers or Takers?

It is a good time to concentrate on what we want our emphasis to be for our families for Christmas this year.

Think about:

Asking family members to agree on a specific limit of gifts to buy for each member, encouraging time spent on homemade gifts and/or commitments of services. Service commitment to be for a minimum of several months so that active giving of one's self is seen as a continuing thing.

As a group (PTL parents, teachers, students), seeking out

CHURCH YEAR
Christmas

the underprivileged and lonely in your community and setting up a continuing plan for active giving in the form of errands, companionship, monetary aid, spiritual needs.

Adults and children setting aside an evening to sing Christmas carols at hospitals and nursing homes. Children's smiles, conversation, and bright faces bring joy to the hearts of the confined. Let's share the joys of our children with them!

In this season, we can help our children develop a faith that is living and active, a faith that encourages them to be givers rather than takers. *(Ms. Betty Brusius)*

Christmas Program Larger Sunday Schools

Having 300 students in our Sunday School has meant that our yearly Christmas program has to be flexible. We have each department choose a song or two that they wish to sing. Learning these songs is all the children do in preparation for the program. During the Christmas program, the youngest children come forward at different times to talk with me about one specific aspect of the Christmas story. This sensitive, touching, and humorous get-together in the chancel brings the children close to me and gets them actively involved in the birth of Jesus through various questions I ask and the conversation that naturally follows.

Hymns, readings, and a short object lesson or puppet show help to pull the whole program together. Preparation by the worship leader takes longer, but the Sunday School children and the staff are saved the burden of extra work during an already busy season. *(Rev. Wayne P. Gollenberg)*

Gifts for the Christchild

Several years ago a lady surprised the church with a Christmas gift of a new piano for the Sanctuary. It really was a surprise! It arrived the Saturday afternoon before the Christmas Cantata, tuned in a key different than the organ. Shiny new and ribbon-bedecked, it sat silent when most needed! Her well-intentioned but

CHURCH YEAR
Christmas

ill-timed gift (she hadn't even told the pastor) caused me to realize that Christ usually takes a backseat to all our friends and relatives on his birthday.

As a result, each December we extend to members and friends of our congregation the opportunity to give "Gifts for the Christchild" at the Sunday morning service before Christmas. In preparation for this event, I make a list of needed items of equipment of furnishings available to the congregation. These have ranged from new hymnals to new pews, from tape recorders to 16mm projectors. Every attempt is made to purchase the item and have it on hand for the Christmas service. Donors give the money to the church, and we purchase the gifts in order to save sales tax and to provide for uniformity and direction.

A lady in the congregation beautifully wraps and displays each package. We also print a special bulletin listing the "Gifts for the Christchild" and the donors. Some of the gifts are memorials, some are in honor of loved ones still living, and others are not designated.

In addition, we provide Christmas gifts, food, and clothing for several needy families each year. Thus people can give "Gifts for the Christchild" in a way that is most meaningful to them. *(Rev. William L. Poteet)*

"Silent Night" By Candlelight

For many years, we have had a candlelight ceremony on Christmas Eve as we sang "Silent Night" at the end of the service. I always enjoyed the effect of seeing candlelight illuminate the faces of God's people. Then I realized that the worshipers themselves could not share this view. This year, we moved the candlelighting ceremony to the reading of the Christmas Gospel. As the pastor proceeded to the center of the church for the Gospel, all turned as in an ordinary Gospel procession. This time the congregation was able to see one another in the beauty of the candlelight. The Gospel reading became a high point in the service and was followed by the singing of "Silent Night" by candlelight. *(Rev. Arthur R. Wilde)*

CHURCH YEAR
Christmas

Christmas "Aid"

Every year our youth decorate the church for Christmas. We now take pictures of the decorations under construction at crucial stages and also take a picture of the whole church after the decoration is completed. It is surprising how much we depend on these pictures every year when it's time to decorate again. *(Rev. Philip J. Bohlken)*

Jesus Meets Santa

Let's face it: the little kids in our congregation believe in that old, red, rascal (Santa Claus), and none of us have the courage to come out and say "there ain't none." This year in our congregation, Santa and Christ confronted each other. During our Sunday School Christmas party (prior to a Sunday morning Christmas program during the regular worsip hour), I played Santa, gave out gifts, and told the Christmas story to kids (seated on the floor). I then attended the service, worshiped the Savior, and listened to the children . . . Santa believes in Christ, too.

On Christmas Eve, I preached a sermon called, "Guess Who's Coming?" I contrasted "the old way with the new" and showed the difference between the stern old morality of the Santa of Germany as captured in the song, "Santa Claus is Coming to Town," i.e., "you'd better not pout . . . he sees you when you're sleeping," etc., with the Christ who brings nothing but forgiveness and acceptance. *(Rev. John Kenreich)*

Spirit of Giving

Last Christmas we tried a new approach in our Sunday School, for we desired to do away with the "what am I going to get" type Christmas. No gifts were exchanged, and no glittering Christmas tree was erected. As we studied the Christmas story about how God cared for us, we made gifts for a refugee family in our community. For our Christmas party, the Sunday School delivered the

CHURCH YEAR
Christmas

gifts to this family and sang carols for them. Then we took the children caroling to the homes of our shut-in members. Our Christmas tree was a large pine near the church on which we strung popcorn, nuts, and berries for the birds. The giving spirit of Christmas was a great success with our children and a most rewarding experience for us all. *(Ms. Linda Lumpkin)*

Not Closed for the Holiday

We generally have a very small attendance at Sunday School on the Sunday immediately after Christmas. Rather than hang out the "Closed for Holiday" sign, we've improvised a family hour for those who choose to come. We sing a few carols, tell the Christmas story or show a filmstrip and then ask the people to divide into groups and make a collage from old Christmas cards on the theme *Christmas Is*. The cards have many beautiful symbols and make an artisitic collage. *(Rev. Gerald L. Mansholt)*

Luther's Christmas Pageant

What we know as "From Heav'n Above" (LBW #51, SBH #22, TLH #85) was written by Martin Luther as a kind of Christmas pageant intended especially for his children. We staged a simple version for our Christmas Eve using a few younger children to act out the roles of the shepherds and teenagers performing as Mary, Joseph, and the Magi. *(Rev. Frederick W. Reklau)*

Theme Trees

Occasionally we like to add a new set of decorations to our Christmas tree. We try to follow a theme. Other years we have used Chrismons, beautifully hand-crafted symbols of Christ; Stars of colored felt stuffed with cotton; God's eyes, (ogoja-dios) in connection with Luminarias; Tree of Death (33 red apples) — Tree of Life, (33 white doves or roses). Watch for decorating ideas on

CHURCH YEAR
Christmas

Christmas cards, in magazines, stores, and garden shops. Keep a file. Create a group of workers. Start early. *(Rev. Richard Hintz)*

Cutting With Current

A few hours before our youth group was to make Chismons, we discovered we could not get half-inch thick styrofoam. We therefore cut the inch thick styrofoam in the following way. I fastened two half-inch spacer blocks to a piece of wood about 20" long, setting the spacer blocks a couple of inches from each end of the board. I twisted two strands of very fine steel wire together before stretching the wire from one spacer block to the other and securing it. With this arrangement, a one amp. trickle battery charger provided just the right current at the six volt setting to cut the styrofoam without melting the wire. The board rested on the styrofoam while I applied a gentle forward pressure. It worked better than I had hoped. *(Rev. Philip J. Bohlken)*

(See FUND RAISING)

CHURCH YEAR
Lent

Easter Prayer Vigil

Our Board of Evangelism planned and promoted a unique Easter Prayer Vigil this year. It began on Good Friday at 9 p.m. (following our Tenebrae Service) and continued until Easter morning at 6 a.m. We posted a sign-up sheet three to four weeks earlier for people to select their times. The prayer times were in half-hour slots, although people could (and did) sign up for more time. The Prayer Vigil was thirty-three hours long, each hour acknowledging one of the years of our Lord's life here on earth. Prayer host/hostesses were there throughout to welcome those coming to pray, hand them a prayer bulletin that gave suggestions for prayer and meditation, and answer any questions that participants might have. They served for three hours at a time.

Those who participated commented that at the next Vigil they would sign up for a longer period of time. More than one person was able to participate during a time period. Sometimes there were four or five people in the chapel. On Saturday afternoon, fifteen of our youth went in together to pray. Many wondered what they were going to pray about for thirty minutes. Afterwards they all said that there wasn't enough time. The altar was bare on Good Friday, with only the Christ Candle lit and small votive candles on the retable. On Saturday evening, the altar was vested for Easter morning. Many commented on the effect the altar and chancel area had on them when they came on Easter morning. It was truly a great spiritual experience for our congregation. *(Rev. William O. Goetzke)*

Views of the Cross

For Midweek Lenten Services, each week have a different person give his/her "view of the cross." Try to pick people with occupations that relate to events of the Passion history. In giving their view, they could refer first to the actual passion event and then give personal testimony about how Christ and the cross relate to their life and work now.

CHURCH YEAR
Lent

For example, here is our Lenten schedule:
Wednesday 1: A Pastor's View of the Cross
Wednesday 2: A Church Treasurer's View of the Cross
Wednesday 3: A Newscaster's View of the Cross
Wednesday 4: A Chaplain's View of the Cross
Wednesday 5: A Lawyer's View of the Cross
Wednesday 6: A Mother's View of the Cross
You could have a policeman, soldier, judge, government worker, doctor, etc. *(Rev. David A. Preisinger)*

Support World Hunger Effort

For our midweek Lenten services, we had soup and bread suppers. Some families were assigned to bring the soup, some the bread, and the rest brought fruit to be shared. Those who did not bring soup or bread contributed to an offering basket for World Hunger. Those who brought food were not expected to contribute anything extra. Each week, the leftover soup was frozen, and on the final evening an interesting *potpourri* was served. We needed only a few extra loaves for this last Lenten meal. These suppers were a rousing success. Most people did not have to worry about cooking a meal before Lenten worship, and hundreds of dollars were taken in for World Hunger. Our Lenten worship began with a fifteen minute hymn-sing followed by a forty-five minute semiformal service. *(Rev. Edgar P. Kaiser)*

Morning Lenten Discipline

An event which complements our midweek evening services during Lent is a gathering at 6 a.m. on Mondays at a local restaurant. We begin with Holy Communion followed by a buffet breakfast. By 8:30 we begin a Bible study. People are free to come and go as their work schedule dictates. Some are able to only attend the communion service. The response for three years running has been tremendous. The event began in an attempt to recapture the "First Day of the Week" emphasis of early Christians. During Holy

CHURCH YEAR
Lent

Week, this schedule is followed every morning. *(Rev. Roy A. Steward)*

Good News From the Pews

For our Good Friday worship service, we planned to read aloud the Passion from John 18:1-19:30. Without some kind of visual help, however, we knew we would lose our listeners after reading only a few verses. So we gathered thirteen volunteers to each read a portion of this Scripture. When their turn came, they simply stood where they were seated, faced the congregation and read loud and clearly. It was very effective. We also did the same thing at the beginning of our Easter worship, reading John 20:1-31 before the first hymn. The Good News gave us something to sing about! To help our readers, we had the entire text typed out with their portions appropriately designated. We plan to do this again. *(Rev. Stephen Miller)*

Lenten Family Fair

What to do when Confirmation Classes are on Wednesday evening and then Lent arrives? Invite the whole family! Gather in the Parish Hall for informal, activity-oriented, family group instruction. Divide all participants into small groups and provide written directions for learning activities. After thirty minutes, journey to the sanctuary for worship. Conclude the evening with coffee and fellowship back in the Parish Hall. *(Rev. L. R. Lineberger)*

Living Lenten Tableau

We asked thirteen men of our parish to grow beards and portray the twelve apostles and Jesus during Lent. At each Lenten service, two of the "disciple" group participated as lectors, giving first-person monologues, etc. On Maundy Thursday, they all distributed the Lord's Supper. A backdrop painted to resemble that

CHURCH YEAR
Lent

of da Vinci's *Last Supper* added to the realism. It was a moving, memorable Lenten experience for our congregation. *(Rev. Arley Fadness)*

Focus on the Upper Room

For the Maundy Thursday service of communion, reenact the preparation for the Passover and the Passover meal using a harmonized account of the Gospel lessons. Use a narrator who reads all the portions between the dialogue. The pastor assumes the character of Jesus distinctly for the purpose of consecration. Twelve others are chosen as the disciples. They assemble from different areas of the church as the drama unfolds. Following the words of consecration, the eleven (Judas has departed) share the communion around a low table set in the chancel area. After the enactment, move smoothly to the full participation of the congregation in the usual manner at the communion rail or around the disciples' table. At the close of the distribution, the person who portrays Judas returns from the back of the church and communes alone. The service is very effective — with or without costumes. *(Rev. Leo E. Wehrspann)*

Lent in the Catacombs

A different approach to Lent is to recreate an early (260 A.D.) worship service. Using the *Didache* and Jewish sources, I developed a service which included Holy Communion, ancient liturgical forms, and the singing of simple psalms. We held it in the catacombs (church basement). Our church provided simple soup; everyone brought bread. We ended by sharing the Eucharist. *(Rev. Jon Erickson)*

Cross Variety

During Lent we made crosses of various styles (Roman, Greek,

CHURCH YEAR
Lent

Russian) for the church walls, cut from homosote (3' x 4') and painted black. A different cross was added each week. They made quite a striking impact by Easter Sunday.

Easter morning, we decorated them with flowers. The following Sunday, the flowers were replaced by large butterflies made from construction and tissue paper. A few Sundays later we had several baptisms, and the crosses were decorated with large scallop shells. When we had a special Sunday School program, we added balloons on sticks. Simulated flames and doves were used for Pentecost. We added another cross on Trinity Sunday, the Jerusalem cross, because the four crosses in the quadrants of the design remind us of the Lord's commission to spread the Gospel to the four corners of the earth. The other crosses were adorned with various symbols for the Trinity. *(Rev. Theodore W. Schroeder)*

(See CHURCH YEAR/Advent)
(See CONFIRMATION/Instruction)
(See FELLOWSHIP)
(See MISSION AND MINISTRY)
(See PUBLIC RELATIONS/Internal)
(See STEWARDSHIP)
(See WORSHIP LIFE/Liturgy)

CHURCH YEAR
> *Easter*

Cross Planting, Part II

Do you remember that great idea in IDEABANK a few years back about planting crosses on every member's lawn on Easter Eve? We tried it and had such a good response that we wanted to do something similar the next year. This time, instead of crosses, we made Easter eggs and went out the night before Palm Sunday. Attached to each egg was a schedule of our Holy Week Services and an invitation to participate. The people are wondering what we'll come up with next. *(Rev. David G. Hungerford)*

Keeping Easter Joy

The Sunday after Easter can sometimes be quite a letdown after the previous week's excitement. On that day, we have a family celebration worship in which everyone participates. The church band helps us with the hymns; we have a puppet show presented by the Youth Group, and we give each person a visual reminder of our worship time together.

One year we collected L'eggs's eggs, decorated them and placed Easter crosses with the resurrection message inside *(available from most Christian book stores at reasonable prices)*. We gave these to the younger children.

Another time we had Sunday School children make multi-colored, tissue paper flowers attaching them to pipe cleaners. We handed them out to everyone who worshiped the Sunday after Easter. During one point in the service, we had everyone come forward to insert their flower into a cross covered with chicken wire that stood five-and-a-half feet high. The flower-filled cross decorated our narthex during the Easter season. *(Rev. Wayne P. Gollenberg)*

Vigil at Sunrise

With Holy Week being so full of special services, we have incorporated the Easter Vigil into our traditional Sunrise service on

CHURCH YEAR
Easter

Resurrection Morning. Since we have a cemetery alongside the church, we begin the worship at the back of the cemetery. An abbreviated form of the Vigil is used which includes: a scripture responsive reading, an explanation of the significance of the Paschal Candle, prayers, the blessing and lighting of the candle, and the sharing of the light among the worshipers as they hold their individual candles. After all candles are lighted, we march in solemn procession to the church. At the church doors, the pastor announces in a loud voice: "Why do you seek the living among the dead? He is not here! He is risen!" To which the people respond: "Amen! Alleluia! Alleluia! Alleluia!" The congregation enters into the church joyfully singing the entrance hymn. At the conclusion of the hymn, a Baptism is performed followed by the reading of the lessons, the sermon, and the celebration of the Eucharist. Communing 150 people, the service can easily be done in one hour. The people love it, and we have a large crowd to participate in the significance of the Vigil and Paschal Candle. *(Rev. Roger W. Bruns)*

CHURCH YEAR
Pentecost

Pentecost Experience

To give our congregation a sense of the first Pentecost experience of many people speaking in tongues, we inserted at random four different Psalms of praise, approximately equal in length, in the Sunday bulletins. Each person, therefore, had one Psalm, and the chances were good that the persons next to them had a different Psalm. At a given time in the service, all the people were asked to read the Psalm, that, in and of itself, was a complete expression of praise. While we read the Psalms we were aware of two things. First, the general confusion of the sound; and secondly, the occasional words of praise we'd hear from the others as they read their Psalms. Despite the general confusion, we could sense others "speaking in our own language." We also gained a strong sense of the richness and variety of this smorgasbord of praise. The spontaneity of this experience was refreshing. *(Rev. David Olson)*

Pentecost Mobile

We used an old discarded lampshade to make a unique Pentecost mobile. After cleaning and painting the frame, we draped red and orange transparent chiffon streamers of various lengths over the frame. Above the frame we suspended a white, descending dove made of inexpensive styrofoam. To bring the mobile to life, we directed an oscillating fan toward it. The streamers made all sorts of dancing movements, suggestive of flames descending from heaven. Playing a spotlight upon it, the mobile glowed with the intensity of fire. It seemed appropriate for Pentecost that we had a moving, active, symbol rather than a stationary banner. The result was interesting and dramatic as well as a reminder that the Holy Spirit is active in our midst. *(Rev. David Olson)*

(See CHRISTIAN EDUCATION/Sunday School)

CHURCH YEAR
All Souls/All Saints/Reformation

All Souls' Accounting Day

This is an effort on our part to know where all of our members are for one Sunday of the year. One month prior to the designated Sunday, we send out a letter to all members explaining our purpose for coming together on this Sunday. (We like to have as many, if not all, of our members present on that Sunday to sing praises to God and to have God speak to them through the Word.) A postcard is enclosed asking for the following information: Will you be in church on this Sunday? (Names of all who will be attending.) If you are not going to be in church on this Sunday, please tell us where you will be. (Names requested also for all those not attending.)

After the due date for the return of these postcards, our elders make follow-up telephone calls to those who have not replied. The result is that we usually have our biggest church attendance on this Sunday. *(Rev. Bill Majer)*

For All the Saints . . .

Every All Saints' Sunday we hang large pieces of poster paper on the walls near the front of the church with the inscription "Our Saints" above them. I ask that each person, upon returning from Communion, write the name of two saints on one of the papers, prefaced by the word saint. The first name written is their own, the other is that of a saint, living or dead, who is dear to that person. It has been helpful for us to broaden our understanding of who saints are and to get a clearer vision of ". . . the holy catholic church, the communion of saints . . . " *(Rev. Robert L. Isaksen)*

(See CHRISTIAN EDUCATION/Sunday School)
(See WORSHIP LIFE/Creative Worship)
(See WORSHIP LIFE/For the Children)
(See YOUTH)

CHURCH YEAR
Special Services

Father's Day Tribute

This is an idea of mine that was well-received in our parish. We inserted a flyer in our Sunday Bulletin several weeks before which read:

IN HONOR OF FATHER'S DAY we will have a special bouquet of flowers on the altar. We invite you all . . . youngsters and oldsters . . . to write a line for your Dad in honor or in memory of him, and we will print it and insert it in the bulletin on Father's Day. A nice way to remember Dad on his day. A donation of any amount ($1, $2, or more) will be greatly appreciated.

Then we asked them to fill out the form below this message noting the amount donated, their message, and their name. Many of our people sent in beautiful messages . . . some were touching . . . some amusing. We plan to do it again next year for both Mother's Day and Father's Day. *(Mrs. Doris Siddon)*

Thanksgiving Giving

Worshipers will be asked to bring to our Thanksgiving Eve service a gift of food to be donated to the poor. It is also the custom of our parish to donate all loose plate cash at this service to World Relief programs — which also contributes to the special character of this holiday devotion. *(Rev. Theodore R. Hanus)*

(See WORSHIP LIFE/General)

COMMUNITY INVOLVEMENT

COMMUNITY INVOLVEMENT

Community Thanksgiving Dinner

During a planning council meeting several years ago, we were looking for specific ways in which to meet the needs of members of our small community. One of the ideas was to have a dinner on Thanksgiving for those who didn't have family or friends or for those who were separated from their family by too many miles. The local community Pride organization enthusiastically gave their approval, and now we co-sponsor a community Thanksgiving dinner. It has truly been an exciting experience. We have residents from the old age homes as well as lonely individuals from our congregation and community. The work that goes into the organization is more than matched by the smiles and comments following the dinner. We ask for reservations through our community paper which makes planning much easier. I highly recommend every community to at least attempt this. It's really been an exciting ministry for us. *(Rev. Kenneth Kaufmann)*

Refugee Real Estate

We sponsored a refugee family and purchased a low-cost home for them. This was financed by $300 loans from individual members with a return interest of 9 percent. The refugee family is renting the house from the church for $150 per month. When the loan is paid off, they will own their home. The notes are payable upon death or demand, and notes are repaid on a lottery basis as money becomes available over and above taxes, interest, and insurance. *(Rev. E. W. Danitschek)*

Adopt a Nursing Home

There are many small nursing homes in our community. Some of the residents do not have families to visit with them. Our Social Ministry Committee decided to "adopt" one such home, with its thirty-one male residents. We decorated the home for Christmas and collected donations of magazines and candy for presents.

COMMUNITY INVOLVEMENT

The Girl Scout Troop had a Valentine's Party for the men. Some of our retired men visit and play cards with the residents. It has turned into an exciting and fulfilling ministry for our congregation. *(Rev. Tim Seeber)*

Hungry Dilemma

Many pastors face a dilemma in attempting to minister to those who knock on the church door claiming to be hungry. Let your congregation budget money to keep the church kitchen stocked with semi-nonperishable lunch items. When someone comes to the door hungry, let the pastor reply, "I was just going to fix myself some lunch. Won't you join me?" or "I'll be having lunch at noon; please join me then." If the word gets out and the church becomes a lunch-haven, so much the better. A new ministry to some of society's outcasts has been started. *(Rev. Monte Luker)*

Castaways for Cash

Living in a climate where there are four seasons, a seasonal thrift shop offers incentive to the congregation to clean closets and also provides a legitimate service to the poor and more frugal members of your community. From such a program, an ongoing ministry might evolve which could continue to be financially supportive of the parish over a long period of time. *(Rev. George F. Lobien)*

(See CHURCH YEAR/Advent)
(See CHURCH YEAR/Christmas)
(See CHURCH YEAR/Lent)
(See CHRISTIAN EDUCATION/Adult Education)
(See FUND RAISING)
(See MISSION AND MINISTRY)
(See WORSHIP LIFE/General)
(See WORSHIP LIFE/For the Children)
(See YOUTH)

CONFIRMATION

CONFIRMATION
General

Confirmands Provide Worship Element

Our confirmation classes make the bread for Holy Communion as one of their final activities before Confirmation. A member of the church who is experienced in breadmaking meets with the class and assists them. By doing this, the confirmands provide a necessary element for our worship life.

This activity also draws the whole congregation together. Not only has the church ministered to its young people by providing Christian instruction, but the young people provide, in the bread, a necessary service to the church. *(Rev. J. Mark Wilburn)*

Salute to Confirmands

Our congregation honors its confirmands each year by preparing a special bulletin board that contains a recent picture and a baby picture of each confirmand. Alongside the pictures are brief resumes of their lives including birthday, baptismal date, schools attended, and hobbies. Confirmation symbols and pictures are interspersed. Featuring the confirmands in this way introduces them to the congregation and makes them feel special on their confirmation day. *(Rev. Kim DeVries)*

Schwichtenbergian Awards

One of the lighter moments in my ministry is the awards ceremonies at the annual confirmation banquet. Several years ago, on a lark, I began presenting the "Schwichtenbergian Awards for Catechetical Excellence." In essence, these are gag gifts to each of the students in the junior confirmation class and, occasionally, the adult class. Some examples of the gifts are awards for the "star pupil" (Christmas star), for the "brightest student" (light bulb), for the student who "kept the class in stitches" (spool of thread and needle), for the student who really used the "old noodle" (bag of noodles), for the student who was really a "chip off the old block" (bag of potato chips), etc. After a few years, the students would talk all year about what their award might be. It is great fun and

CONFIRMATION
General

demonstrates that Christians need to use and develop their sense of humor. When I recently accepted a call to another parish, at the farewell the last catechism class presented me with an award for "Catechetical Teaching." It was for the instructor with a lot of "snap, crackle, and pop." The award was a pan of Rice Krispies bars. *(Rev. Willis R. Schwichtenberg)*

Capturing History

I often find that in many churches there are display cases for trophies and plaques but seldom have I seen display boards for past confirmation classes. Group pictures are always taken at that time of the year, and perhaps it would be of some value to frame these for the hallway of the church to emphasize the history of Christ's people. *(Rev. Edward Arle)*

(See CHRISTIAN EDUCATION/Adult Education)
(See FUND RAISING)
(See FELLOWSHIP)
(See WORSHIP LIFE/Lent)

CONFIRMATION
Instruction

Tying It Together

How to end catechetical instruction and prepare youth for the Rite of Confirmation (Affirmation of Faith) is always a puzzle. Oral or written exams tend to strike fear in the youth; they reward memorizers and emphasize knowledge as a prereqisite. To emphasize confirmation being a stage in our journey of faith and an opportunity for the youth to share their faith, I require three things of each confirmand: (1) An essay on the topic, "What My Faith Means to Me," which is printed in the bulletin on the day of Confirmation; (2) a project of their own choosing — banner, poster, mobile, poem, essay, etc. (with my approval) — that expresses some aspect of their faith life; (3) a personal interview with me to discuss their life with Christ. I encourage one or both parents to be present for the interview. These three things give each young person an opportunity to think about and personally express their faith. *(Rev. Michael Blackwell)*

Confirmands Project Faith

In January our eighth grade confirmands begin personal projects to express their faith. They are subsequently shown and explained on Confirmation Day. Adult members work with the young people on a one-to-one basis to build relationships as well as to help get the projects completed. We encourage the young people to use their own special talents and interests in selecting a project. Some of them have been: posters, banners, a huge wooden cross, string art in various colors, playing a flute piece, rug-hooking, photography. The congregation becomes more interested in Confirmation Day as they look forward to seeing the individual statements of faith. After Confirmation, our church building is decorated with the various projects. *(Rev. Mikell Peratt)*

Confirmation Entrance Exam

What do you do about the confirmation student who runs to Webster's Dictionary when you ask him to look up John 3:16? Or the one who thinks you're talking about a new soft drink when you

CONFIRMATION
Instruction

mention Moses? We don't have this problem, because everybody must pass a Confirmation Entrance Exam before they begin their confirmation instruction.

One year before the children start their confirmation instruction, they are told: "If you want to start confirmation next year, you have to pass the Entrance Exam. Here's a study guide that will help you. All the answers to the tests are in this study guide." The guide includes the Ten Commandments, the Apostles' Creed, the Lord's Prayer, the books of the Bible in order, instructions on how to find biblical references, and a summary of salvation-history beginning with Abraham.

Students take the exam in the spring before they are to begin confirmation instruction. Those who have been faithful in Sunday School attendance usually find it a snap. Those who have not attended regularly usually fail. They are given a second (or third . . .) try at the exam after further study and special assistance from a tutor. The good news is that *everybody* (so far) has passed the test. The best news is that the students actually learn the material, and we don't have to turn our confirmation classes into a futile exerise in remedial instruction. *(Rev. John E. Priest)*

Confirmation Research Paper

To help our children grow in faith and spiritual knowledge, each confirmand is challenged to complete a ten-page handwritten research paper using the Bible and other resource books. Thirteen weeks before confirmation, we ask them to choose three items of interest from a list of approximately twenty subjects. I assign one topic from the three they've selected. The papers are corrected and returned to the confirmands who then condense their work into one page for presentation at Questioning Night prior to confirmation.

The most surprising thing is that the young people not only know what they have to do, but they are *anxious* to get started. When they present their papers on Questioning Night, they serve as excellent teachers to those present because they understand what they are saying. *(Rev. William R. Voelker)*

CONFIRMATION
Instruction

The Long Arm of the Lord

Include a pre-arranged visit to your local police station and an interview with a willing policeman as part of your confirmation instruction. Our kids have a study of the Fourth Commandment and Romans 13. The police are surprised to find out that God is supporting their lonely work. The kids get the full treatment: a trip to the jail, fingerprinting, and a tour of the station. *(Rev. Mark Spelzhausen)*

Peer Ministry

Our young people in grades ten through twelve are invited to take part in our CONFIRMATION CATECHUMENATE — a year long preparation for final initiation within the Roman Catholic community. This year, we invited some of the confirmed teens to come back again as sponsors for this year's candidates. The sponsor's role is that of peer minister — one who intercedes in prayer for his/her candidate; one who makes the journey with the candidate. Sponsors also facilitate discussion, act as counselors, help evaluate the candidate's readiness and, finally, present the candidates to the Bishop for Confirmation. *(Sister Marguerite Stapleton)*

Discipling Disciples

When making hospital or shut-in calls, take another person along. Many have already done this, but when you include confirmands who may not be able to see where discipleship really fits into their way of life, it can be especially helpful. It might also serve to create new interest in other areas of church life and pave the way for greater involvement. As I once read, "The youth are not the church of tomorrow, they are the church of TODAY." *(Rev. Edward J. Arle)*

Lenten Overnight

During the Lenten Season with all its pressures, I disband my confirmation classes and hold an overnight retreat at the church

CONFIRMATION
Instruction

instead. It runs from Friday evening until Saturday afternoon. We accomplish the same six hours of class work. The new format provides a needed change of pace, and we find we are able to build group cohesiveness. Generally, we concentrate on one topic and use a variety of creative ways to enhance our learning together. *(Rev. Mark Bauer)*

Confirmation in the News

Discover Bible commentary from the comic strips. We help the students identify biblical concepts that are discussed in the comics. A study sheet is supplied with an example. The list includes sin, guilt, forgiveness, grace, peace, calling, obedience, joy, etc. Discover Bible commentary also in the daily news. We have our students look for articles of controversial character of real life drama that allow them to apply Law and Gospel. *(Rev. Mark Spelzhausen)*

Media Aids Confirmation

We check the TV guide for possible films or documentaries that may be valuable teaching aids for our confirmands. They report back on the TV program with help from a study sheet. *(Rev. Mark Spelzhausen)*

Featuring Funnies

Cartoon strips clipped from daily newspapers can be excellent teaching aids. Many illustrate truths about human nature with wit and wisdom and often have much to teach about our relationship with God. I have written a series of youth confirmation lessons using a cartoon strip as a rib-and-thought tickler for the preface to each of thirty lessons. "Peanuts" "Hagar the Horrible" "Boner's Ark" and "Cathy" are some I find most usable. Consult your local newspaper on arrangements for permission to reproduce this copyrighted material. *(Rev. Frederick W. Reklau)*

CONFIRMATION
Parental Involvement

Confirmation: A Graduation or a Beginning?

For the past couple of years, I have played a "values clarification" game with the young people who were about to be confirmed and their parents. We have an evening reception a couple of days before Confirmation, and the main activity consists of this game which enables the confirmands and their parents to better understand the importance of Confirmation. It also strives to facilitate the sharing of options with each other.

The game consists of three parts. First, I have them stand in the middle of an open room and make an either/or choice over some non-threatening ideas such as, "At this point in time do you feel more like a roller skate or a pogo stick?" The purpose of this activity is to get them to loosen up and to begin to share their feelings with one another. The second part consists of the same kind of either/or choice, but this time choosing between two different definitions of Confirmation. I have developed ten different statements about Confirmation, all of which have some validity, and they are asked to choose one or the other. Then they explain to each other why they made that choice. Finally, having placed numbers one through ten around the room, I give each of them a sheet on which is printed the ten different definitions of Confirmation. They are instructed to stand under the number of the definition which best fits their feeling about Confirmation. Once they have made their choice, the parents and confirmands are told to find the other members of their family and meet in neutral territory to try to arrive at a concensus for their family. This has produced not only interesting discussion that evening but discussion that carries forward in the days following. *(Rev. Wayne C. Schroeder)*

CONFIRMATION
Rite of Confirmation

Confirmation Reminders

In our church it is traditional to assign confirmands a Bible verse at the time of their Confirmation. The verse is selected with each student in mind and read aloud at the Rite of Confirmation. Two years ago, I started reinforcing that procedure by presenting a poster to each confirmand with their Bible verse printed on it. Most hang them in their rooms, and they serve as a visual reminder of the day long after it has past. *(Rev. David G. Hungerford)*

Confirmand's Own Banner

We confirm on Pentecost Sunday, and one of the things the young people look forward to most is having their own Confirmation banner hanging in the chancel. The women of our church (usually parents of the confirmands) design and make the banners, each with a symbol of the descending dove of the Spirit, and the first name of each confirmand. After the service, the confirmands take their banners home along with their gifts from the congregation. In subsequent calls in members' homes years later, I have seen these banners still hanging proudly on the wall. *(Rev. Joel J. Brauer)*

EVANGELISM

EVANGELISM

Fishers of Men

To stimulate our members into thinking about evangelism, and to help them overcome their reticence to actually make an evangelism visit, we initiated a special emphasis. On a large bulletin board, a fishing net was hung over blue paper with the caption, "I WILL MAKE YOU FISHERS OF MEN." We encouraged members to take the paper cut-out colored fish we provided, to think of someone they know (neighbor, friend, or relative) whom they would like to receive an evangelism call, and to write information about this individual or family on one side of the fish. The fish are posted on the bulletin board, information side down. The Evangelism Committee, using these fish, compile a new list of people who are visited in a special evangelism calling program. *(Rev. Richard J. Foss)*

Getting the Message on Cable TV

Local cable systems may provide opportunities to schedule religious programming. We made arrangements for VHS cassettes of *This is the Life* to be telecast twice weekly in our community at 6:30 p.m. *(Rev. David H. Preus)*

Love Lifted Me!

Have each person write a Scripture reading on "love" on a small piece of paper. Insert the paper into a balloon. Fill each balloon with helium gas, and send the balloons aloft on February 13. The messages will be received on Valentine's Day. *(Miss Pat Hunsuck)*

> *(See MISSION & MINISTRY)*
> *(See PUBLIC RELATIONS/Internal)*
> *(See PUBLIC RELATIONS/External)*
> *(See WORSHIP LIFE/General)*
> *(See WORSHIP LIFE/Advent)*
> *(See WORSHIP LIFE/Lent)*

EVANGELISM

FELLOWSHIP

FELLOWSHIP

Modern Cana Feast

Come to the "Cana Feast!" Our youth annually sponsor a Valentine's Dinner [ed.'s note: Could also be done in the wedding month of June.] for married couples in our congregation. We call it a "Cana Feast" which connects it with the famous wedding at which Christ was present.

The youth fix the food for the dinner, provide entertainment, and decorate appropriately with hearts and flowers. Entertainment has included skits with a romantic turn, songs like "Do You Love Me?" from *Fiddler on the Roof,* and other romantic ballads. We seat the couples according to the month of their wedding anniversary and have them share any humorous events that occurred in connection with that special day.

Finally, the evening ends with a brief service of reaffirmation of their marriage vows which one of our pastors conducts, more special music (including songs which are often used by people at their weddings), and the order of service printed in a wedding service folder. *(Rev. Margaret L. Rickers)*

Salt Shakers

We have a get acquainted organization called Salt Shakers that meets one evening a month in parishioners' homes for an informal dinner and Christian fellowship. Our coordinator picks the hostess each month from the list of interested people. She also gives the hostess three other signed-up couples (or singles) to call and invite to her home. The hostess decides the menu and the time. She prepares the main dish and asks the other three couples to bring the side dishes (salad, dessert, rolls, etc.) Each month the coordinator tries to get a hostess and couples together that have not met before. Sometimes the coordinator may ask the hostess to invite a couple she thinks may be interested in joining Salt Shakers. Our group has been a fine resource for getting members to know each other better. *(Rev. R. M. Hagestuen)*

Mardi Gras Perks Up a Parish

Experiencing a doldrum atmosphere in the parish last fall, we

FELLOWSHIP

struck on the idea of holding a Mardi Gras before Lent. Much planning was done for months. Our people responded beautifully. The whole parish — youth and adults — shared in the preparation activities. No fund raising was involved, but there was a charge for the dinner-dance in the evening. It was so much fun; we are making this an annual event. *(Sister Agnes McLoughlin)*

"The Other Alternative"

With the help of a sister congregation, we have operated a successful young adults' coffee house, "the Other Alternative." Our coffee house is open one night a week to all teenagers and young adults in the area. We have a diverse group and find that college students often stop in whenever they are home for vacations. It's one place they can find some old familiar faces. Several participants bring guitars or other musical instruments. We also bring our own refreshments and clean up the room after the gathering. Attention is focused on the love of the Lord through folk singing, rap sessions and Bible studies — all dedicated to finding the strength for our lives through Jesus. The group usually numbers twenty to twenty-five. Through the coffee house, we are offering a place where young adults can find friendship and look to God as a guide for their lives. *(Mrs. Jean Stevens)*

Mother's Day Dinner

What to do on Mother's Day? Our local men's club sponsors a dinner on Mother's Day that really does give mom a day off. They buy ice cream, bread, salad and potatoes and bring several outdoor grills to church. Each participant brings their own meat and $1.00 to cover the costs. Because we have quite a few single adults, we invite them to come for free. They bring their own meat but that's all. The men do all the work and mom really gets a day off. *(Rev. Kenneth Kaufmann)*

(See ADMINISTRATION/General)
(See CARING MINISTRIES)
(See CHRISTIAN EDUCATION/Adult Education)
(See CHURCH YEAR/Advent)

FELLOWSHIP

(See CHURCH YEAR/Lent)
(See SENIOR CITIZENS)
(See WORSHIP LIFE/Music, Choirs)
(See YOUTH)

FUND RAISING

FUND RAISING

"What Shall I Render to the Lord . . ."

Because most youth group activities cost money, we spend ample time raising funds for our various activities. We have added an important dimension to these money-makers. We give 10 percent of our earnings to missions. In one case, funds for evangelism supplies were provided to a sister congregation just beginning a new outreach program. Fund raisers are now more than just money-makers. The kids have fun and they learn valuable lessons in stewardship. *(Rev. Robert Kuupler)*

Shoot'em-out Fund Raiser

For two years our church has successfully involved all age groups in a mission effort built around the recreation program. The event, called a Deacon/Staff Shootout, is a basketball game staged each year on a Friday in mid-November to avoid local football schedules.

The co-ed basketball game pits the church staff against the board of deacons with both teams hamming it up as much as possible. Cheerleaders, half-time events for the children, free throw contests, craft and bake sales are just some activities which complement the game. Admissions and proceeds from the entire event go to world hunger or local missions. This is a fun evening for all ages that is highly anticipated each year for the fellowship it provides and the cause it supports. *(Rev. Glenn Davis)*

Penny Stack

An easy, lucrative, and fun fund-raiser which can involve your whole congregation is called a penny stack. Everyone has extra pennies in their pockets on a Sunday morning — including the little youngsters. Encourage them to add to the stack.

Choose a distance which is significant to your project. For example, our youth are shooting for collecting half-mile of pennies because our departure point for an upcoming trip to San Antonio

FUND RAISING

is approximately one-half mile from church. Would you believe one mile of pennies equals in excess of $10,000? Therefore, our kids have a goal of about $5,000 in pennies to raise for their trip.

Provide a clear plastic container which is accessible to all in the narthex, so that everyone can observe your progress. I'd suggest frequent emptying of the container (and recording of its contents) to avoid leading anyone to temptation. *(Margaret L. Rickers, D.C.E.)*

A Mile of Coins

One busy day at a shopping center, a Scout troop asked passersby for pocket change to help them string out a line of coins, edge-to-edge and back and forth, across a portion of the large parking lot. They explained that half the proceeds would go for the troop and the other half for a worthy cause. Moving toward the target distance excited interest and involvement. *(Rev. Frederick W. Reklau)*

Gift Book

When we were building our new church, rather than placing individual plaques on everything, we publicized gifts for specific parts of the new Sanctuary (pews, altar, windows, etc.) in a permanent Gift of Remembrance book which is now kept in a special place in our narthex. *(Rev. Richard Klabunde)*

Gone But Not Forgotten

Write all former members giving them an opportunity to help in raising money for a given project. Many former members may still have strong attachments to the church and like to feel a part of what goes on there even though they have moved away from the area. *(Rev. Michael Lutz)*

FUND RAISING

Bricks for Peace

At Peace Lutheran Church, where we began a program of building expansion, one fund raising idea was called "Bricks for Peace." We provided ceramic brick-shaped banks for people to fill for the building fund. These banks were made by a member and had a felt covered opening on the bottom so the contents could be removed without breaking the bank. To pay for materials and also provide income for the building fund, a donation of $10 was asked for each brick. The gold bricks were sold out before the article about them even hit the church newsletter. *(Rev. Arthur R. Wilde)*

Turn the Tree Green

A large tackboard placed in a high traffic area like the narthex had a bare-limbed tree drawn upon it. A sign invited people to turn the tree green by thumbtacking either dollars (of any denomination) or change in green envelopes to an empty place on a branch (tacks and envelopes were available). *(Rev. Frederick W. Reklau)*

So Much Per Mile

Have a walk-a-thon where individuals get sponsors for any amount per mile. The more people you have, the more sponsors you have, the more income you will receive. This is also a very enjoyable activity for young and old together. To encourage people to have many sponsors, give mementoes of the event for getting specific numbers of sponsors. Have a special prize for the person with the most sponsors and also one for the most amount of money received. *(Rev. Michael Lutz)*

Raising Christmas Trees

Our church has about ten acres of property on the outskirts

FUND RAISING

of the city. We plan to order Christmas tree seedlings this fall and plant them next spring. With additional plantings each year, spraying for diseases and insects, and proper pruning, our first crop should be ready to harvest in three to five years. Our yield will probably be about 500 trees a year. We plan to give the trees away in exchange for a free-will offering to our church, and to sell decorations, lights, and ornaments at the same time. We anticipate that the whole project will generate quite a lot of funds for our efforts. *(Rev. Rod Broker)*

Fill the Coin Barrel

A small barrel with a clear, plastic top having a coin slot could be placed in a high-traffic area such as the narthex. Invite people to FILL THE BARREL! As an additional interest-sustainer, Sunday School children could be offered a prize for guessing closest to the actual amount when the barrel is filled. *(Rev. Frederick W. Reklau)*

(See ADMINISTRATION/General)
(See COMMUNITY INVOLVEMENT)
(See STEWARDSHIP)
(See WORSHIP LIFE/Music, Choirs)
(See YOUTH)

MISSION AND MINISTRY

MISSION AND MINISTRY

Bringing Mission Closer to Home

Sometimes in a rural ministry, people find it hard to envision parts of the world where their benevolence dollars go. To help close this gap, we have brought guests into our parish from hundreds and even thousands of miles away. Expensive? If you think $10 to $35 per visit is expensive, then perhaps it is.

There are not any expensive travel or lodging arrangements involved. In fact, our missionary guests come to us via the worldwide telephone network. Our local Northwestern Bell office provides free use of their amplified-conference phone systems. These permit over 100 worshipers to listen in on proclamation being shared miles away from their dairy farms and small Main Street businesses. The units also contain a microphone so that our guests can listen to our end of the celebration as well.

This inexpensive visiting method has enabled us to stay in touch with our missionaries in Indonesia. Last Maundy Thursday (Good Friday morning over there), the sermon was delivered from a distance of over 10,000 miles away. "Ma Bell" did much to erase any feeling of distance.

No longer do we hear the comment, "Where is that benevolence money going anyway?" *(Rev. Jack Richards)*

Visiting Together

Our parish evangelism committee proposed and helped carry out a joint evangelism visitation project with our sister United Church of Christ congregation. Using local government maps, we listed every home in the community. With trained teams of one Lutheran and one United Church of Christ member, we visited all the homes in our community. Together we produced a brochure that we used during the visitation and later placed in public places. Both parishes received new members through our joint effort. *(Rev. John M. Aurand)*

Increase Mission Support

During Lent, we distribute dime folders to our members. Before that, at our January Voters' meeting, everyone chose six spe-

MISSION AND MINISTRY

cial charities to support. We discovered that involvement in the selection increases the amount for these charities threefold. When the dime folders have all been brought in during Holy Week, we tabulate the total and divide the amount received by six, the number of charities that the congregation chose. *(Rev. William R. Voelker)*

Sharing Garden Surplus

As harvesting begins, parishioners bring surplus garden foods to an area of display at our church. Those who can use fresh vegetables are invited to take what they need — first come, first served. The takers simply put a free will offering into a market container. The entire collection is sent to ELIM (Evangelical Lutherans in Mission). We recommend this practice to churches whose members grow vegetable gardens. *(Rev. Raymond G. Moelter)*

Soap for Missions

Local motels are often willing to save used soap bars left by guests. Check with the manager or the head of housekeeping. Inform them that the soap will be sent to World Relief. A responsible collector can pick up the soap according to the motel schedule — maybe on a monthly basis. We collected 140 pounds in three months. *(Rev. Dr. Peter Mealwitz)*

(See ADMINISTRATION/General)
(See CHURCH YEAR/Advent)
(See FUND RAISING)
(See PASTOR/PARISHIONERS RELATIONSHIPS)
(See NEW MINISTERS (MEMBERS))
(See STEWARDSHIP)
(See WORSHIP LIFE/For the Children)

NEW MINISTERS (MEMBERS)

NEW MINISTERS (MEMBERS)

New Kind — Two Kinds

We have solved the problem of membership in our church for the many people who live north in the summer and south in the winter. Our regular membership is the same as that in any other church, but we offer an alternative. PLC (Participating Lutherans for Christ) membership is suggested for those who wish to keep their communicant membership in their home church. PLC's are not counted in our statistics but may hold office, use offering envelopes, attend the Lord's Supper, and take advantage of all the rights of regular communicant members along with all the duties and responsibilities involved. Regular membership is encouraged for all who live in our area at least six months of the year, but for the others who are here for only three to five months, we feel we are better able to serve their spiritual needs in this way. This arrangement need not only work for "Sunbelt" churches but for other vacation area parishes too. *(Rev. John F. Meyer)*

"The Lord Is My Shepherd"
But Someone With Skin on Helps Too

Happiness is finding a new church and feeling secure and loved. Our Lord has always sought after his lost sheep, and he uses us, his children, to help the lonely and hurting within our churches. In our moves about the country, we have felt this love through several shepherding programs. At one church new members were welcomed at a Sunday evening tea. As we stood in the reception line, our shepherd couple introduced us to the congregation, telling us about certain members who had similar interests. As time went on, they continued to keep us informed of all church gatherings and made an effort to drive us quite often. They have remained our friends, and we keep in touch though we're not miles apart. Another church assigned shepherd leaders for groups in areas. In this way, we became acquainted with people in our vicinity. We attended group meetings for the purpose of discussions on the purpose of the church, prayer, and what it means to be a part of the Body of Christ. Some nights we dispensed with the study and had

NEW MINISTERS (MEMBERS)

a cookout or potluck supper. The shepherds kept a close watch on their group to prevent anyone from being lonely or in need of help. Shepherding can work in any organization of the church — singles can pair up as shepherds as well as married couples. They should be responsible to the church board. Shepherds need to be mature people in the faith, and need to be compassionate, caring, and be truly interested to tackle the job seriously. Any program can become boring if the people in charge lose their pep and excitement. One person's response to a shepherd call was, "I am unable to come because of my health but please keep calling. It makes me feel as if I have a friend." *(Mrs. Joan Martin)*

Welcome New Members

One way to expand your lay leaders' ministry and also provide a positive experience is to have them visit new parishioners. To each new member, our deacons bring a packet of materials which includes: a parish roster, the year's calendar, vital statistics, questionnaire, offering envelopes, parish brochure, and a variety of pamphlets. The visit is easy and helps make the new member feel welcome. *(Rev. Henry Simon)*

(See ADMINISTRATION/General)
(See CHRISTIAN EDUCATION/Adult Education)
(See YOUTH)

PASTOR/PARISHIONERS RELATIONSHIPS

PASTOR/PARISHIONERS RELATIONSHIPS

The Telephone "Call"

In a day of working parents, shift schedules, outside activities, television priorities, and shut-ins who are not home, the pastor may well use the telephone for many "calls." In a half-hour during early evening, I can contact seven to ten homes with words of congratulation, of happiness at a return from the hospital, of condolence for a relative's death, of concern for a sick person, of awareness that a person has been absent from worship, etc.

The telephone "call" shows a responsibility of pastoral care. Brief in words, it may well end with a spiritual tone, such as: "God bless you," "I pray for your good health," etc. It does not take the place of home visits, but it may be used in many circumstances, saving time and gasoline. *(Rev. Peter Mealwitz)*

Discussion-in-the-Round

The results of a pastor's counseling, planning sessions, and one-on-one brief discussions held in a pastor's study are usually greatly improved if everyone present (including the pastor) can sit around a circular table in the study. The table may be small, but it does do the following: 1) the pastor is more likely to be viewed as a helper instead of the boss; 2) people feel a little more secure because the lower half of their body is behind the table; 3) the pastor can actually be nearer to the others as they talk across the table; 4) people feel more comfortable being able to lean on a table; 5) a table with paper and pencils available encourages people to take notes so they don't forget what they said they would do. *(Rev. Robert Floy)*

Pastoral Personals

Try a column in your newsletter where you aren't preaching. I call mine, "thoughts WHILE BY MYSELF . . ." Every now and then remind your readers that these are simply thoughts, nothing more. It will allow you to gripe, laugh, poke fun at the world (not *your* members). It's great therapy for letting off steam. *(Rev. Bernard W. Johnson)*

Visual Reminders

For home and hospital visitations, I use an assortment of colorful cards (purchased from the Hermitage Art Company, 5151 N. Ravenswood Avenue, Chicago, Illinois 60640). On the back of the picture card I type various Bible verses appropriate for different situations. During my visit, as I share in devotion and prayer, I read and refer to the Bible verse. After the devotion, I leave the card with the typed Bible verse as a visual aid for further contemplation. Children and the aged especially love the cards and will place them in their Bibles, on dressers, or on window sills. *(Rev. Roger Hoffman)*

Say Thanks!

I keep a supply of seasonal postcards in my desk drawer. The day after a special event or the very day a gift is given to the church, I write a one or two line thank you to the person who has contributed a talent or a gift. The colorful postcard plus the pastor's personal "noticing" keeps pastor/parishioner lines open. *(Rev. Dr. Peter Mealwitz)*

Postals to Parishioners

To contact church members who may need a little encouragement to worship regularly, we send a personal, caring message on a postcard which features a picture of our church. *(Rev. Lyle Rich)*

Late Callers

When the phone rings in the middle of the night, have your wife answer it. She can calmly schedule an appointment for 9 a.m.

PASTORS/PARISHIONERS RELATIONSHIPS

the following day, refusing to wake you. There isn't much good you can do at 2 a.m. (i.e., explaining to an alcoholic why his wife is leaving him) unless it is actually an emergency. *(Rev. Bernard W. Johnson)*

(See ADMINISTRATION/General)
(See CARING MINISTRIES)
(See WORSHIP LIFE/General)

PUBLIC RELATIONS

PUBLIC RELATIONS
Internal

A New Slant

When I need to be sure that a certain article is read in our newsletter, I sometimes type the first paragraph on a slant. The visual attraction is enough to catch members' attention . . . and that's half the battle. *(Rev. James R. Pierce)*

Fill in the Blanks

Most congregations publish a monthly activity calendar. Rarely are all the spaces filled up with lists of activities or events. We try to fill these blanks with quips, prayer needs and requests, Bible quotes, or suggestions such as: "Invite a friend or neighbor to worship with you tomorrow;" "Have you spent time with God in prayer today?"; "Have you read your Bible today?" The possibilities are as varied as your imagination. Many of our parishioners keep their calendars in the kitchen, and we know they are used and looked at frequently. *(Rev. Lester Messerschmidt)*

"Lite Brite" Draws Attention to Coming Events

It may look like a touch of Las Vegas, but it works! When we had trouble getting people to sign up for certain events, we decided to "put it up in lights." Using a Lite Brite toy, we made a border of red and gold and inserted a sheet of paper on the board with the announcement we wanted to highlight. Using an interrupter plug, we made the outside border lights blink on and off. It was a real eye-catcher, and it reminded people to sign up before or after the service for an activity they might have otherwise forgotten. *(Rev. David Ethan Olson)*

Advance Notice

It isn't unusual for congregations to put out a flyer or brochure

PUBLIC RELATIONS,
Internal

advertising their Lenten series of meditations. Why not continue the practice throughout the year?

Using our Easter banner design on the cover, we printed the lessons for the Easter season and the theme for each Sunday of Easter. This helps prepare the congregation for worship and seems to enhance the worship life of the congregation. We hope to have a flyer depicting the Sundays of Pentecost ready for distribution toward the end of the Easter season. It is a good way to look ahead at the lessons and to show the continuity of the church year and the Scripture readings. *(Rev. Dennis M. Drews)*

Old Bulletins Never Die

Many churches use Sunday bulletins that contain a meditation based on one of the lessons for the day. I file these by text. When the text rolls around in another three years, I may have a sermon starter right at hand. Most bulletins also have a handsome picture on the front cover which is also related to one of the texts. I save these too. There might be a sermon starter in one of them, or they can be used for a bulletin board or other visual display.

Another good use for old unused bulletins *(like those that go through the mimeograph unprinted)* is for personal correspondence. One never knows how the Spirit works, and the recipient of the letter just might appreciate a Gospel message along with the letter itself. *(Rev. John H. Leitel)*

Loose-Leaf Church Books

We publish our church's annual reports and yearbook in loose-leaf form *(punched on the side to be inserted into a notebook)*. We have found this to be very helpful. In this way, we can update the books by sending out new pages with our newsletter. These are then inserted into the books. We also print our Constitution and By-laws in loose-leaf form and encourage all of our organizations to do the same so that everyone has all their church-related

PUBLIC RELATIONS
Internal

material in their own personal binder. *(Rev. Gary S. Coble)*

Members in the News

People like to see themselves in print. We feature a picture page every month in our church paper of members at work in the parish. *(Rev. Lyle Rich)*

(See ADMINISTRATION/General)

PUBLIC RELATIONS
External

Extra! Extra!

The local newspaper can serve as an excellent vehicle for the gospel in both small towns as well as in larger cities. Churches have not been creative enough in their use of this media. For your consideration:

- Get acquainted with your local newspaper's editor — or the religion editor.
- Submit articles about your church's activities. (Keep them short and to the point . . . it's also free advertising.)
- Most small town papers do not have a religion editor. Discuss the possibility of your filling that void with the editor.
- Consider writing a religious column for your paper on a weekly or bimonthly basis. (I wrote a religious column called "Eusebius" for the local paper in Perryton, Texas. The editor was happy to have a free writer.)
- Discuss with area pastors/laypeople the possibility of publishing an inter-Lutheran newsletter/newspaper. Exposure of the church through your efforts might enhance Christian unity within your community. Area churches could underwrite the first few month's issues with paid advertising a future option. The paper could serve as a clearinghouse for local and national Lutheran activities as well as a forum for dialogue. *(Rev. Thomas W. Schaefer)*

Canvass By Mail

You can reach 1,000 homes with information or evangelism literature for approximately $35 in postage. Make use of a bulk mailing permit. Your city directory provides names and addresses of residents. A group of parishioners can address the mailing as a fellowship project. People like to receive mail. Door knob hangers seldom get inside the door. *(Rev. Dr. Peter Mealwitz)*

(See ADMINISTRATION/General)
(See MISSION AND MINISTRY)
(See PUBLIC RELATIONS/Internal)

SENIOR CITIZENS

SENIOR CITIZENS

Helping Elderly Worship

Many older parishioners are unable to participate in worship because of the weight of the hymnal. When my mother mentioned this to her pastor, he made a point of Xeroxing the whole service — hymns and all — for Mom. Instead of a two-pound hymnal to carry, Mom now has only three or four sheets of paper. *(Rev. Donald F. Hinchey)*

(See CARING MINISTRIES)

STEWARDSHIP

STEWARDSHIP

Money-back Offer for Potential Tithers

Some people honestly believe they cannot afford to tithe. They are convinced that this is simply beyond them. They would find, were they to try it just once, that tithing is within their capability and can become for them a source of immense blessing.

Lent is a season for self-denial. "Tell me," people wonder, "how does God want me to deny myself?" Easter is a season for celebration. "Tell me," they ask, "how can I significantly celebrate our Lord's Resurrection?"

I suggest that you encourage your congregation to consider combining these two special seasons with the contrasting moods *(six weeks of Lent and seven of Easter)* to make a one-quarter year trial period for tithing. Combining self-denial with celebration, they are to set aside the first one-tenth of their March-April-May income for the Lord's causes. By the time Pentecost arrives, their answer will be clear: some will want to go on doing this, and others may find it is not meant for them.

At the end of the thirteen weeks, if your people decide tithing is not for them, simply tell them to stop giving for a while, until the calendar catches up with what they have already given. That will not be difficult. And everyone will be able to say, "I gave tithing a fair try."

Of course many will want to continue tithing. I would also suggest a short personal testimony, such as:

"Years back, someone asked us to try tithin. Our salary then was $2,000 a year, with family on the way. We began. And ever since, through years of booming babies, teenage appetites, college tuitions and four mission churches started from scratch, we have never stopped being blessed. And so we never stop appealing to friends, young and old, single or family: Try it, please. Try tithing. There is no other way you can really know whether this may be God's special blessing for you." *(Rev. A. K. Boehmke)*

Talent Bank

Stewardship programs often only emphasize the stewardship

STEWARDSHIP

of financial resources. As part of our annual Stewardship Program, we distribute Commitment Sheets to all communicant members. The Commitment Sheet lists all the formal programs of our congregation, as well as personal, devotional, and worship opportunities. We ask members to mark all the items to which they would like to commit themselves for the following year. These sheets are collected and kept by a People Resource Person appointed by the Board of Stewardship. They form the basis of our talent bank.

When planning a particular program such as VBS, we have a list of people who have indicated interest in it on their Commitment Sheets. The sheet is tailored to the varied opportunities for mission and ministry in our congregation. At the bottom of the sheet, the people may write any talent or interest they have which is not currently a formal part of our congregational program. It is amazing to discover the resources available in a relatively small group of people. *(Rev. Ronald K. Heimsoth)*

Interest Free Loans

Ask members of the congregation to make interest free loans to the parish which will be returned upon demand. These loans would be placed in high, interest-bearing, money market funds. If a significant amount of capital is invested at 10 to 12 percent, the return could be appreciable. It is also possible that some of the parishioners will allow the church to keep the money they have placed on deposit after they have been living without it and its earnings for a while. They would be able to list the amount donated as a tax deduction. *(Rev. George F. Lobien)*

Special Appeal

Use all special offerings (Christmas, Lent, etc.) for special causes in the benevolence area. People are more generous in supporting causes. If you have a special need for the church, make a personal appeal for donations of $100. Publish that the money is not coming from the church's general fund but from people giving sacrificially. In this way, we raised $1,350 to facilitate our participation in the Bethel Bible Series. *(Rev. Bernard W. Johnson)*

STEWARDSHIP

Personalized Stewardship Program

Take 25-35 slide photos of the parish during the year *(youth meetings, Ladies Guild, people at worship, Christian education classes, etc.)* and then tie it together with a twenty-minute tape presentation. This makes for a very personal stewardship presentation where the people can see themselves in action. To further the mission theme, add pictures of other churches and pastors in your district. *(Rev. Donald Beyer)*

(See ADMINISTRATION/General)
(See CHRISTIAN EDUCATION/Sunday School)
(See CHURCH YEAR/Christmas)
(See FUND RAISING)
(See MISSION AND MINISTRY)
(See SENIOR CITIZENS)
(See WORSHIP LIFE/General)

WEDDINGS/MARRIAGE

WEDDINGS/MARRIAGE

Wedding Music Aid

The persistent problem of young, to be-wed couples not knowing good and appropriate wedding music and hymns has been solved by our organist. We now have a cassette tape featuring various musical pieces for organ and guitar, and a number of solos by two soloists in the congregation. The couples can now listen at their leisure and pick selections that they like. *(Rev. Carl R. Sachtleben)*

Marriage Enrichment Event

Due to the increasing costs of utilizing motels or retreat centers, our congregation is planning an outdoors enrichment event for married couples. Couples will provide their own tenting equipment, (the church will assist those without sufficient or suitable equipment). All large group sessions will be scheduled under the shelter, with couple interactions allowed anywhere outside or in the tents. We feel that the combination of bringing couples together in this manner will prove an excellent opportunity for nurture and reawakening of their marriages. Couples will take turns preparing the meals. *(Rev. Scott Hawkins)*
(See FELLOWSHIP)
(See PASTOR/PARISHIONERS RELATIONSHIPS)

WORSHIP LIFE

WORSHIP LIFE
General

Interpreting Worship for the Hearing Impaired

You may be surprised at how many hearing impaired people there are in our own community! On the first Sunday of each month we offer a sign language service of Holy Communion for the hearing impaired. We have not only aided the hearing impaired in "hearing" the Good News but have helped some of them to find a sense of community beyond that of other hearing impaired persons. It has also wonderfully enriched our congregation's sense of ministry to the whole person, in a very visible way. And I have learned to keep my sermons clear and simple! *(Rev. Joel J. Brauer)*

Devotional Tape Ministry

We are presently developing a devotional tape ministry in which different families of the congregation will prepare a week's worth of devotions on tape. Each family will be provided with an outline to follow, suggested themes for the church year, how to begin, how long each devotion should be, etc. These tapes will then be duplicated and distributed to members of the congregation on each Sunday. This idea originated out of a Planning Council Retreat where it was expressed that more of our members need to hold family devotions. Included in the church budget is a tape duplicator, a supply of blank tapes, and a number of tape players for those families who neither have one nor can afford to buy one. Before someone can pick up a new tape, they must bring back the tape from the previous week. *(Rev. William O. Goetzke)*

Involving Laity in Worship Planning

Our Worship Committee is recruited monthly by the elder who is serving as assisting minister for the month. From his Shepherding Responsibility List, he usually selects two couples and a single or youth. They meet with the pastor and the elder for several sessions to study the lessons for each Sunday of that month. Out of this comes not only hymns for the day, sermon thoughts for the pastor, variety for the order of worship, Bible study for the par-

WORSHIP LIFE
General

ticipants, but an enthusiasm for what goes into worship and into the planning. Most who have participated are eager to do it again. They get to pick some of their favorite hymns, hear some of their thoughts come out in the pastor's sermon, and just enjoy contributing personally to the joy and meaning of worship. There is also less complaint about hymns "we can't sing." *(Rev. Robert J. Schrank)*

Quick Communion Bread

- 3 cups self-rising flour
- 3 tablespoons sugar
- 1 12-ounce can of beer *(any brand)*

Mix ingredients; pour into well-greased loaf pan; bake at 350 degrees for fifty minutes. That's all there is to it. Makes a tasty loaf of bread that can be used for any occasion. *(Rev. Jon Fogleman)*

Communion Cup Preference

Some of our members prefer receiving Holy Communion from glasses while others prefer the common cup. To solve this problem at our church, a small table is set with individual cups in a place where parishioners pass it on their way to the communion rail. During the distribution, the host is distributed by an elder. The pastor carries the chalice, and an acolyte follows along with a wine-filled cruet. As the pastor approaches each celebrant, if they are holding a cup, the acolyte fills it from the cruet. For the others, the common cup is offered. This is done easily and successfully at our Eucharist services and is an aesthetically-pleasing solution. *(Mrs. Shirley Morrison)*

Communing the Alcoholic

Our altar guild provides grape juice for alcoholic members who commune with us. However, unrefrigerated grape juice begins to ferment. We solved our problem by freezing the juice in small cube trays, then only removing as many cubes as are needed for the service. It saved us dollars and steps. *(Rev. Mark Pries)*

WORSHIP LIFE
General

Moment on Worship

In two congregations where I served, I have had a "moment on worship" every Sunday in which I explained different aspects of worship. In one parish I began with the principal parts of the interior of the church building, in another I started with the explanation of the *Lutheran Book of Worship*. There was always something that would come up that required explanation on the basis of conversations with members. An annual favorite in years gone by was the explanation of Septuagesima, Sexagesima, and Quinquagesima Sundays. Some "moments" were also repeated every year. *(Rev. Howard A. Kuhnle)*

Greeting Visitors

For immediate reference, I keep a 3" x 5" card in my hymnal on Sunday. Before the service, when visitors are introduced to me, I quickly jot down their names and the name of the member with whom they came to church. After the worship, I can glance at the card to recall their names as I greet them when they are leaving the church. *(Rev. E. W. Danitschek)*

Agriculture Sunday

Along the lines of Rogate Sunday in the old lectionary, each spring when the farmers in our rural parish plant corn, I have a service of blessing of the seed. I share the seed with the youth during the children's sermon, commissioning them to plant the seed. Later in the fall, we celebrate the harvest at Thanksgiving by providing flour for a needy family. *(Rev. James Butt)*

Bulletin Fillers

I find that the rubrics of the hymnal make excellent Sunday bulletin fillers. Each week a given "direction" assists the worshiper in better understanding the worship service. *(Rev. Dr. Peter Mealwitz)*

WORSHIP LIFE
General

Assisting the Guest Minister

Whenever I arrange for a guest minister, I provide "tools" to assist his/her presiding at the service. At least two weeks prior to leading the worship, we mail the service schedule for the day, a copy of that Sunday's CELEBRATE, a current worship folder, and a step-by-step directive sheet of the liturgical service conducted at our church. Guest ministers feel more comfortable, and they enjoy their presiding because of our efforts. *(Rev. Dr. Peter Mealwitz)*

Welcome at All Doors

In retirement, I serve as part-time visitation/supply/interim pastor in various congregations. When I began as the associate pastor of visitation at one large church, I went to the main door of the church and joined the pastor to greet the people after the close of the service. However, we were actually in one another's way. After a few Sundays, I noticed that some parishioners left the church by way of a smaller, secondary door. This did not give the pastor a chance to greet these people. After consultation with him, we decided that I should stand at this smaller door to greet those who were leaving, and I also had an opportunity to greet those whom I would not otherwise have met. This plan may be a good suggestion for other associate and assistant pastors. *(Rev. Howard A. Kuhnle)*

Bigger Than Life

Despite the protests, everyone likes to see their name or picture displayed. During special services, I have used slides of the congregation as a visual message. On Thanksgiving we will use some current slides of people who are serving in the congregation. In this way the names in the bulletins can be associated with the slides of those people. *(Rev. Steven Rice)*

Lite Hymnals

We have found that the size of the LW or LBW and its weight

WORSHIP LIFE
General

are two problems facing some people because of physical handicaps. For those with arthritis or other similar problems, we have provided them with copies of the liturgy and hymns taken from the hymnal. Each person has expressed their gratitude for our thoughtfulness. These stapled copies are provided by the ushers to those whom they feel or know will need them for the service. They are then returned for use in another service. *(Rev. Steven Rice)*

(See ADMINISTRATION/General)
(See BAPTISM)
(See CHRISTIAN EDUCATION/Sunday School)
(See CHURCH YEAR/Advent)
(See CHURCH YEAR/Lent)
(See MISSION AND MINISTRY)
(See PUBLIC RELATIONS/Internal)
(See SENIOR CITIZENS)

WORSHIP LIFE
Creative Worship

Double Bible Class Attendance

Use a combined worship and study session. A thirty-minute worship period (including a ten-minute sermon) is followed by forty minutes of Bible study, closing with the prayers for the day and the Benediction. Dismiss children for Sunday School as the adult Bible study begins. Holy Communion is celebrated fifteen minutes in advance of the Worship time. Parents with small children love the service and keep their children in church for the thirty minutes, before going to Sunday School or Nursery. This program is most effective for the early service on Sunday. A full-length service follows for those who prefer regular worship. Never have so many been so willing to participate in both worship and Bible study. Try it, you'll like it. *(Rev. Paul G. Hansen)*

An Eye for Imagery

Visualize psalms in worship by using slides which correspond with the images given verbally in the psalm. Appropriate music can enhance the total impact. *(Rev. David H. Preuss)*

Celebrate Sunday School!

One of our fall worship services centered on parish education to celebrate the 200th anniversary of our Sunday School. Teachers from Vacation Bible School and Sunday School wore blue anniversary ribbons stating, "I Teach," and all students wore similar ribbons in red, stating "I Learn." The church was decorated with streamers, balloons, and a Sunday School anniversary banner. A special anniversary design with the words, "Sunday School — It Makes a Difference," was printed on balloons given to each worshiper.

Following our morning worship, we served a potluck dinner in honor of our teaching ministers. We also had a special two-tier cake frosted with the anniversary logo, in the colors used on the

WORSHIP LIFE
Creative Worship

banner. A festive spirit abounded, and it was enjoyed by all. *(Rev. Thomas A. Damrow)*

Vocational Garb Sunday

Luther stressed that every vocation should be a Christian vocation. A few years ago at Reformation time, we asked the members of the parish to come to church dressed in their normal, everyday work clothes. People came in nurses' outfits, bakers' aprons, hard hats, greasy mechanics' clothes, in farmers' biboveralls, just to name a few. We also wrote a special service dealing with the topic of one's "vocation/calling." It was great and did much to help everyone's self-image. Everyone could see himself or herself as a vital part of the Kingdom of God at work Monday through Friday. *(Rev. David A. Peters)*

(See CHRISTIAN EDUCATION/Adult Education)
(See CONFIRMATION/Instruction)
(See CHURCH YEAR/All Souls, All Saints, etc.)
(See CHURCH YEAR/Christmas)
(See CHURCH YEAR/Lent)
(See CHURCH YEAR/Easter)

WORSHIP LIFE
For the Children

Children's Sermons for Everyone

The regular Sunday morning homily can be given added zest and interest by occasionally using props which are suggested in the many books on children's sermons. The authors of these sermons often do a good job of highlighting the central theme of a text with some prop: a bag of groceries, a toy car, a few easily drawn signs, a shoe box, etc. The skillful preacher can apply these ideas for the entire congregation without making them seem juvenile. Oftentimes the use of props will involve members of the congregation and will bring the preacher out of the pulpit and into closer contact with the people. *(Rev. Roger W. Bruns)*

A Magical Mission

To help emphasize Mission ministry I have used a magical trick. I choose one that is not too complicated for my children's sermon. After I have amazed the children and parents I call the children into a huddle and explain the message of how the trick was done. Their assignment is to share with the congregation in their own way how it was done. I tie this into the message of Good News in Jesus that we share each Sunday. This message we should also reveal to others in our own way. *(Rev. Steven Rice)*

All Hallows Eve for the Children

In order to counter the false teaching on Halloween, we designed a church-time program using the theme "Hooray for the Saints!" to correlate with the original idea of All Hallows Eve. Our main Scripture text was Hebrews 11, which lists many of the great Biblical saints and their exploits. In addition to singing and stories about some of these saints, the children were instructed in making bread dough figures of these men and women of God. After baking the figures, painting them, and rehearsing something of that person's faith, the children displayed them and took them

WORSHIP LIFE
For the Children

home to mount. On the final Sunday the children joined the congregational worship by contributing a song, "And I Mean to Be One, Too", in honor of the saints. *(Rev. Scott Hawkins)*

Bless the Children

Many congregations invite their non-communing children to come forward at the time of the distribution for a blessing. We have slightly altered that concept so that they come forward after the distrbution has been completed. This eliminates the need for those distributing the Sacrament to remember who has and who has not received their First Communion. In addition, the children seem to take a special pride at the separate recognition given them at this time. It has been a source of deep meaning for members of the parish to see the eagerness with which the children come forward. *(Rev. Edwin K. Rehrauer)*

Puppet Preaching

Wanting to have something special for the children of our congregation on Sunday mornings, I write a play each week based on one of the lessons from the lectionary series. In a simply constructed puppet theater at the front of the church, we act out the play.

We have found the puppets to be a blessing. The children love them, and the adults are crazy about them, too. A puppet's preaching often gets the message across in a profound way. *(Rev. Gary S. Coble)*

(See CHRISTIAN EDUCATION/Sunday School)

WORSHIP LIFE
Liturgy

Family Assistance at Worship

We ask entire families to serve as assistants at Sunday worship. The family works it out among themselves who will assist with the various parts of the liturgy. In this way, we have children and parents participating in those portions of the service recommended for assisting ministers. They may chant or speak the Kyrie, introduce the Hymn of Praise, read lessons, lead prayers, gather and present the offering and Eucharistic elements, and distribute the bread and wine. Every family of our church is offered the opportunity to minister the Sunday worship, and the concept has been well received. *(Rev. Rod Broker)*

Scriptural Liturgy

Parishioners are often amazed to find that the words of the liturgy are both scripturally based and are often direct quotes. Prior to a season such as Advent, Lent, or Easter I may devote the entire worship service to "Bible References in the Liturgy." The service is printed with the Scripture passages noted. *(Rev. Dr. Peter Mealwitz)*

WORSHIP LIFE
Music/Choir

Having Fun with the Hymnal

When our congregation purchased new hymnals, there was an outcry of frustration over new hymns, changes of words or tune, and elimination of some old favorites. We made several attempts to deal with these problems, including some fairly traditional approaches: hymn of the month (to introduce a new hymn), historical sketches of hymns, discussion of words, and brief rehearsals on difficult passages. However, a more enjoyable and amusing approach has been informal games based on hymns. This works best at family nights, Sunday School, and at youth activities. "Name That Tune" has been a popular game in which we give clues about a certain hymn and ask competitors to bid a note (i.e., "I can name that tune in five notes . . . four notes . . . three notes, etc.) Of course, it is helpful when there is some familiarity with the words, tune, or background of the hymns. "Take Five" is another fun strategy. A hymn number is chosen at random (by drawing, three rolls of dice, or whatever), and then we sing that hymn and the next four that follow in the hymnal, whatever they may be. Sometimes we struggle through one or two, usually we find we like at least two or three of them and often make the pleasant discovery of a fine hymn. To acquaint younger people with the titles and words of hymns, "Charades" and "Password" also suggest enjoyable games. And once the title is guessed, a verse or two can be sung. *(Rev. David Ethan Olson)*

Speech Choir

When I became Pastor of this congregation, we had a very small choir with great limitations. We began to use speech choirs for liturgical parts of the service — which the choir might otherwise have sung — for verses, offertories, responses. No musical talent was required, although at times we accompanied the speech choir with instrumental music. A wide variety of ages could particpate, and the effect was exciting and uplifting. Now we have a larger choir, but on Reformation Sunday we used a speech choir again. It rehearsed church history as an introduction to the service.

WORSHIP LIFE
Music/Choir

Martin Luther even said a few words. We plan to keep using two kinds of choirs now! *(Rev. James G. Bauman)*

To Sing or Not to Sing

In every hymnal edition there are those singable and those unsingable hymns. My desk hymnal is coded A, B, and C as to the singability of hymns. Some hymns may be sung with alternate familiar tunes, which are so noted. A few hours spent with a pianist in marking the hymnal provides easy access to Sunday hymn selection for the season of the year and for themes. The B category denotes hymns for learning. Also, a choir can be of assistance in introducing new melodies. *(Rev. Dr. Peter Mealwitz)*

For Your Listening Pleasure

In order to raise money for new robes, our senior choir is making a tape which we will duplicate and offer to the congregation for donations. It will contain anthems used in our worship services. Before making the tape, we are asking our members to suggest favorite anthems they would like included. The tapes will also be given as a gift to each of our shut-ins. *(Rev. Timothy J. Fangmeier)*

Hymns Recorded for Pastor

Our organist is tape recording every hymn in the Worship Book. When I select a hymn, I can easily check out the tune by playing the cassette. *(Rev. E. W. Danitschek)*

Sing a New Song

Tired of reprinting new hymns each time you want to sing one? Or having supplemental songbooks that fall apart or need to be

WORSHIP LIFE
Music/Choir

added to regularly? We have solved the problem by hanging a projection screen in the church where it can be seen by all. New hymns are typed in large type (IBM's Orator) and then transferred onto overhead transparencies. You can obtain overhead blanks to use on every type of photocopy machine, which gives you a permanent overhead. The overhead projector is placed on a front pew, and the room does not need to be darkened. The transparencies are easily stored and can be reused. Our collection of hymns is now well over 100 and gives a greater variety to our singing and allows for old favorites not in current hymnals. *(Rev. Douglas Webb)*

(See CHURCH YEAR/Christmas)
(See FUND RAISING)
(See MISSION AND MINISTRY)

WORSHIP LIFE
Prayer

Prayers for All

How often do we reserve prayer in the church service only for those who are sick and injured while the healthy and the whole never get much attention? Besides the prayers for those needing special attention, each week include a prayer for a particular family in the congregation. Families are called to mind in prayer for their welfare and in Christian appreciation of their being part of the community of Christ. Often a family will be caught off guard by the surprise of hearing their name mentioned just for being Christ's children. A further benefit is that delinquents are called to mind as well, and this may serve to awaken concern for those no longer part of the active community. In addition to this, the congregation might be asked to remember in prayer throughout the week each of the families mentioned. The name and address of the family might also be highlighted in the bulletin. *(Rev. Edward Arle)*

People Pray

One month prior to Advent we invite laypersons to offer their own General Prayer at worship from Advent through Pentecost season. Guidelines are sent out for the preparation of the prayer asking them to prepare about 200 or 300 written words. They offer their prayer at the services they attend; the pastor offers the prayer at the other services. Many wonderful prayers are offered! *(Rev. A. F. Volmer)*

(See BAPTISM)
(See CARING MINISTRIES)
(See CHURCH YEAR/Lent)

WORSHIP LIFE
Sermons

Sermon Preparation

Some time ago, two colleagues and I retreated to a mountain cabin for two days of long-range sermon planning. We brought along resources, previewed and discussed upcoming texts, and provided for individual reading time. Each developed individual charts to view the four months ahead and jotted notes for each week's text, themes, key words, illustrations, resources, and children's sermon ideas. The effort paid off. Sermon preparation became better organized, joyful, and productive. *(Rev. R. Gregg Kaufman)*

For Those Who Want More

The priest in our parish writes notes for his homily. He then makes available a resume of the notes. During the homily, he mentions that a reprint containing more information on the topic is available in the vestibule. We run 200 copies. They are gone in no time. *(Sr. M. Joan of Arc, SND)*

WORSHIP LIFE
Summer Worship

Summer Sermon Spin-offs

During the summer when many of our teachers and students are vacationing and traveling, our church school classes that follow Sunday morning worship are replaced by "Sermon Spin-offs." In an informal atmosphere with coffee and cookies available, the preacher leads a discussion of the day's worship theme. It's a wonderful opportunity for sermon dialogue. I've also found that many illustrations which didn't quite fit into the sermon work themselves out nicely in these gatherings. *(Rev. David A. Roschke)*

Summer Family Fellowship

Concerned with the problem of poor attendance at Sunday worship and Sunday School during the summer months, our congregation canceled Sunday School and held a Wednesday evening family fellowship and learning program during July and August.

We spent forty-five minutes playing various games for all ages, had a refreshment period, and an hour long educational activity. While children attended puppet-making, story telling, or music, adults watched a slide tour of the Middle East, had a three-week discussion on the synodical merger, and experienced other forms of adult education.

Some of our evenings entire families gathered for a swim party, a movie, or a barbecue. Every week we closed our fellowship with worship.

The benefits proved to be very positive. Children especially looked forward to coming to church for the special activities, and adults gained from the fellowship and relaxed learning atmosphere. *(Ms. Lael Cordes)*

Worship on Track

Trying to add some variety to our summer worship services, I based my sermon each Sunday around printed tracts which I ordered from either Concordia Tract Mission or the American Tract

WORSHIP LIFE
Summer Worship

Society. Each worshiper takes the tract home as a reminder of the message. *(Rev. Timothy J. Fangmeier)*

YOUTH

Christmercials

If you have any kind of Rally Day, Talent Show, Church Anniversary, or whatever coming up, be sure to give teenagers a chance to write some commercials for it. Most of them watch too much TV, so why not put their abuse to good use. Have them use tunes and situations from TV ads and re-write them as Christ-centered messages. The youth will have a ball writing, editing, and acting in them; and you'll be amazed at the results. Here's one example from our youth (to the tune of *Look for the Union Label*).

> *"Look for the love of Jesus, when you are looking for something worthwhile. Remember always, the love of Jesus. When you have problems with daily life and want some help you know he is always with you to lead you safely through good times or bad. So always look for the love of Jesus. He's got you with him and will never ever let you go!"*

On one Sunday evening, our group came up with twenty-two "Christmercials" — the possibilities are enormous . . . and the fun's not bad either. *(Rev. Wayne P. Gollenberg)*

Human Sexuality Classes

Is sex education being done well in the schools in your community? As a church, we sponsored an "Introduction to Human Sexuality" that we think is a model program for providing good sex education. We invited youth in grades five to twelve and their parents to four consecutive Monday evening sessions. Topics were: "Anatomy and Physiology" and "Teenage Pregnancy" (all age groups), "Dating and Emotions" (grades seven to twelve), "Love and Marriage" (grades nine to twelve), "Growth and Development" (grades five to six), and "Family Unity" (grades five to eight). We used films, speakers with expertise in particular aspects of human sexuality, and discussions led by the speakers and other selected leaders.

The films and discussions were frank, open, and sensitive. The young people appreciated being able to talk about sex in a co-ed

YOUTH

setting. To encourage questions, we had everyone submit an evaluation/question and comment sheet. The discussion leaders then answered these questions.

The program was well received. There were 200 to 250 participants each evening (in a community with a four-year high school of about 250 students). *(Rev. David R. Aaseng)*

Handicap Awareness Retreat

Our youth have mini-retreats or "all nighters" as the kids call them. They come for supper, camp out on the floor in the basement, and leave after breakfast. One theme we used this past year was a surprise. As the young people came in, each one was given a handicap, especially suited to the person. The one who talked the most was given a stroke (taped mouth, tied hand and leg on right side). The football hero ended up in a wheelchair borrowed from the ambulance service. Others lost hands (tied in socks), or were blind, used walkers, crutches, etc. We continued with our regular evening. We had games, Bible study, discussion, made and ate pizza and popcorn (a real job for the blind and those without hands). At midnight we had a healing service including communion. As each person received the elements, they were also healed (tape removed, untied, etc.). We then talked about handicapped persons, our own health, and the meaning of the Sacrament. It was one of the best youth meetings of the past year. *(Rev. Jon Erickson)*

Fellowship for Kids

Because our congregation is large, many of the children attend different schools and live in different neighborhoods. When they reached junior and senior high school age, it was more difficult to form a strong youth group because the personal relationships had simply not had time to develop in many cases. To try to improve this situation, we formed a **Fellowship for Kids** ministry that included all children aged three to twelve. We planned monthly activities, publicized them well and invited every child. Activities and events have included a halloween Party, Harvest Festival, Thanksgiving Feast, Christmas Decorating, Valentine Party, Lent

Event (at which children made Lenten banners), Easter Party, Field Day, picnics, and field trips. Occasionally we had special games for different ages (preschool, primary, and intermediate), but most of the time all ages participated together. *(Rev. Richard J. Foss)*

Spend Money on Youth

Rare is the church that reaches all its youth by youth meetings and activities. Even though our youth activities are quite well attended, we also give a yearly subscription of *Campus Life* to each of our post-confirmation youth and a subscription to HIS (published by the Inter-Varsity Fellowship) for the college age group. This supplies each teenager or young adult with relevant Christian literature even though they may never attend a youth gathering. The cost is high (around $10 per person each year), but we spend more than that each year for Sunday School material. Why not spend some money on the post-confirmation youth? *(Rev. Lester Messerschmidt)*

Bike Tune-up Day

Interested in finding a way to make an impact on the youth of the community, we decided to have a "Bicycle Tune-up Day" in our parking lot and publicized this in the local newspapers. We enlisted the help of a local bike shop owner and another professional who handles large groups of youth with weekend Motocross bicycle races. On the day itself, there were displays, an ongoing demonstration of trick riding by a bicycle Motocross team, and examination of the bicycles along with suggestions for tuning and adjustments. Our youth group served refreshments, and Scripture portions and tracts were provided at the serving table. One man, whose son got involved, spoke to me about some real personal needs. Apparently his trust level had been heightened as he saw the church's interest in meeting his son "where he was at." *(Rev. John V. Herrmann)*

Christo-Lanterns

Our junior youth class brought gutted pumpkins into class.

YOUTH

After our Halloween party, they formed small groups with each group having a pumpkin. We gave each group a topic *(Christmas, Good Friday, Easter, Pentecost, etc.)* and asked them to carve a symbol in the pumpkin for the event and give a summary of the event. We sat on the floor with pumpkins glowing for our closing devotions. Each group gave their presentation and led the whole group with one verse of a meaningful hymn for the occasion. We have also done this with the closing at a congregational party having youth and adults working together in small groups. *(Rev. Dan Wehrspann)*

Luther Service Awards

While I was a pastor at Ascension Lutheran Church in Milwaukee, Wisconsin, we instituted the Martin Luther Award. This is given once a year by the youth of the church to adults who have gone far beyond the call of duty in serving youth. Presentations were made at a youth banquet where Lutheran materials and decorations gave identity to the occasion. We held the event as close to Reformation Day as possible. Since a number of adult guests were invited, no one knew who the recipients of the awards would be except a small youth committe and the youth director. Usually we gave three to five awards each year; two to the youth for outstanding service and three to adults. *(Rev. Hoover T. Grimsby)*

(See BAPTISM)
(See CHURCH YEAR/Advent)
(See CHURCH YEAR/Christmas)
(See CHURCH YEAR/Lent)
(See CHURCH YEAR/Easter)
(See CHRISTIAN EDUCATION/Sunday School)
(See CHRISTIAN EDUCATION/Vacation Bible School)
(See CONFIRMATION/General)
(See CONFIRMATION/Instruction)
(See FELLOWSHIP)
(See FUND RAISING)

MISCELLANEOUS

Blue Jeans Sunday

In order to get all the spring cleaning done without the same few people doing all the work, we have established "Blue Jeans Sunday." Chairpersons are selected for the various projects. All materials (such as cleaning compound, wax) are purchased. We ask people to bring shovels, rakes, hedge trimmers, and to come in their work clothes — "grubbies" — blue jeans! We have an outdoor worship service from 9-9:30 a.m. on the church lawn. After worship, each chairpersons asks for volunteers for their project. At noon, all work ceases. One year we had a potluck. Last year, the church provided the lunch for everyone. The fellowship is terrific. The work gets done, and all feel they're part of the church. *(Rev. Thomas A. Herbon)*

Passage Key

It is distressing to strike gold only to later lose the location of the find. When you find an especially helpful insight to a biblical passage, note the source and page number next to the passage in a wide-margin, study Bible. Provide yourself with a key to your abbreviations inside the front cover of the Bible. Some of these insights will be even more profitable if they are referenced under the appropriate entry in your Bible dictionary or in your commentary. This process saves you time and becomes a reference to your whole library as well as reinforcing the frailty of memory. It also delights later since you've gathered a wealth of impressive references with almost no effort. *(Rev. Philip Bohlken)*

Need Slides?

Put a basket in the front entrance of the church after you have requested slides through parish publications and/or pulpit announcements stating your needs (e.g., nature, family, action). It worked for us. *(Sr. M. Joan of Arc, SND)*

Recycle Religious Programs

Check with a nearby radio station which broadcasts the Lu-

MISCELLANEOUS

theran Hour or Portals of Prayer. They may be happy to give you the records after their use. These can be distributed to shut-ins or can be used for your own devotional life. The music portion can be transcribed onto a cassette for developing music appreciation in confirmation classes. *(Rev. David H. Preuss)*

Searching Out Resources

I have devised a RESOURCES SURVEY under the topics of Worship, Nurture (Education), Fellowship, Mission, and Service. Once a month I sit down with a brother clergy and pick his brain for resources, ideas, etc. that have worked well for him. It's amazing the resources I've uncovered. *(Rev. David C. Schroeder)*

Archive Volumes

At the end of each year, we have a full set of all Sunday and other worship service bulletins bound for the parish library archives. This provides historically valuable data. We also do this with our parish paper and our annual parish report. These three items provide vital data for practical parish usage through the years. *(Rev. Fred D. Dommer)*

Family Scrapbook on the Wall

We designed a picture-frame board of plywood with grooved wood strips to hold polaroid snapshots of members, visitors, and special events. Our "Trinity Family Scrapbook" is on the wall of the room where we hold the Sunday morning coffee hours, and each week our "cameraperson" takes a few snapshots of the worshipers. This also lets the visitors know they are important to us, and members become familiar with new people to whom they were just introduced. *(Rev. William Beck)*

Recovering the New Testaments

In recent years, our paperback copies of *Good News for Modern Man*, which we keep in our pews for worship, have become shoddy and worn. Rather than throw them out or store them away where

MISCELLANEOUS

they'll not be seen (or used) again, our Ladies Association has been re-covering them by using 8½" x 11" bulletin covers (with a picture that covers one whole side) that we had leftover from Easter and Christmas festival services. They cut them to size and glue them over the old, worn-out covers of the books. The new covering not only reinforces the old covers but provides a new seasonal picture which brightens the book's appearance. *(Rev. William Shimkus)*

Rotating Church Library

Paperback book carousals *(like the kind used in bookstores)* can be placed in the narthex holding books from your church library. People are more apt to take the time to look at this display than go into the library. Make it easy for them to check out the books by themselves — a simple signout sheet would do. You may have a few books stolen, but more will be reading, learning, and returning. *(Rev. Bernard W. Johnson)*